ADVANCE REVIEWS BY OTHER PUBLISHERS

"I enjoyed reading <u>The Nuclear Devil's Dictionary</u>, and my assistant did as well. . . . The subject and approach (not to mention the cartoons!) are perfect for a mass audience, but the writing style is too sophisticated for that same audience."

"Although I am in complete sympathy with the dictionary you want to publish (and think the material you sent is excellent) I don't see the book for our list."

"It's apparent you've done a great deal of work on this, and I certainly appreciate your direction. [But] humor and satire in general are having a tough time of it around here, and your book would start off facing some pretty stiff opposition."

"I don't feel it has the kind of broad commercial appeal we look for with our titles although I do admit the material is timely."

"<u>The Nuclear Devil's Dictionary</u> is an admirable idea. My personal reaction to it is that the terminology is so unremittingly technical and horrific that it defeats any attempt to transform it by satire or wit. It's not a book that [my publisher] would do."

"<u>The Nuclear Devil's Dictionary</u> is a fine idea and I enjoyed reading it. Unfortunately, . . ."

The Nuclear

Devil's Dictionary

The Nuclear

Devil's Dictionary

by

James J. Farrell

Usonia Press   Minneapolis

Acknowledgments:

From <u>Feiffer</u>: <u>Jules</u> <u>Feiffer's</u> <u>America</u> <u>From</u>
<u>Eisenhower</u> <u>to</u> <u>Reagan</u>, edited by Steven Heller.
Copyright (c) 1982 by Jules Feiffer. Reprinted by
permission or Alfred A. Knopf, Inc.

Description of nuclear explosion reprinted by permission or Grove Press, Inc. Copyright (c) 1982
by David P. Barash and Judith Eve Lipton.

Cover painting by Janine Applequist.

Cover collage by Jennifer Lee.

Cartoon on back cover reprinted by permission of
Tony Auth, Philadelphia Inquirer.

Usonia Press
Box 19440
Diamond Lake Station
Minneapolis, MN 55419

EVOLUTION

DANA SUMMERS/*Fayetteville Times*

On the 40th anniversary
of Hiroshima and Nagasaki,
this book is dedicated to
the victims of nuclear war,
past, present, and future.

"But 'glory' doesn't mean 'a nice knockdown argument,'" Alice objected.

"When I use a word," Humpty Dumpty said in a rather scornful tone, "it means just what I choose it to mean-- neither more or less."

"The Question is," said Alice, "whether you can make words mean so many different things."

"The question is," said Humpty Dumpty, "which is to be Master--that's all."

Lewis Carroll
<u>Through</u> <u>the</u> <u>Looking</u> <u>Glass</u>

Introduction

In his 1946 essay on "Politics and the English Language," George Orwell claimed that "there is no such thing as keeping out of politics. All issues are political issues, and politics itself is a mass of lies, evasions, folly, hatred, and schizophrenia. When the general atmosphere is bad, language must suffer." "In our time," Orwell asserted, "political speecn and writing are largely the defense of the indefensible. . . . Thus, political language has to consist largely of euphemism, question-begging, and sheer cloudy vagueness."

Orwell's 1984, published three years later, described a world in which the major powers "continue to produce atomic bombs and store them up against the decisive opportunity which they all believe will come sooner or later." In the novel, Orwell introduced Newspeak, a language devised to ensure unthinking acceptance of the status quo and the arms race. The philologist Syme tells Winston, the protagonist, that revisions in the language "narrow the range of thought. . . . The Revolution will be complete when the language is perfect. . . . Orthodoxy means not thinking. Orthodoxy is unconsciousness." In an appendix, Orwell provided "The Principles of Newspeak," a language designed "to provide a medium of expression for the world-view" of the State, but also "to make all other modes of thought impossible."

Orwell assumed that language both contained and conveyed meaning: "if thought corrupts language," he said, "language can also corrupt thought. A bad usage can spread by tradition and

imitation, even among people who know better."
But Orwell did not consider the situation hope-
less; he believed that "the present political
chaos is connected with the decay of language, and
that one can probably bring about some improvement
by starting at the verbal end. If you simplify
your English, you are freed from the worst follies
of orthodoxy." Although this dictionary does not
deal with questions of syntax or grammar, it still
hopes to free readers from the follies of orthodoxy.

Although it owes much to Orwell's insistence
on clear thought and communication, it owes as
much to the American writer Ambrose Bierce. As a
San Francisco journalist, Bierce occasionally
inserted satirical dictionary definitions in his
columns. These definitions exposed the assumptions of Americans by showing the gulf between
rhetoric and reality. For example, Bierce defined
"language" as "the music with which we charm the
serpents guarding another's treasure," and he
tried to expose the deceitful charms of language.

In 1906, Doubleday, Page and Company published a short collection of these definitions as
The Cynic's Word Book. In 1911, Bierce included
The Devil's Dictionary in his collected works,
dedicating it to "enlightened souls who prefer dry
wines to sweet, sense to sentiment, wit to humor,
and clean English to slang." In 1967, Doubleday
published The Enlarged Devil's Dictionary, including 851 additional definitions that Ernest Jerome
Hopkins had culled from Bierce's newspaper
columns. In all this work, Bierce was a consum-
mate cynic, which he defined as " a blackguard
whose faulty vision sees things as they are, not

as they ought to be." This dictionary aspires to a similar faulty vision--to see things as they are, in order to imagine things the way they ought to be.

The method is quite simple; The Nuclear Devil's Dictionary merely translates the vulgar vocabulary of nuclear newspeak into common English in order to keep us all from being lexi-conned by the powers that be. It is meant to be both consciousness-raising and conscienceness-raising, and informative in the full sense of the word: conveying knowledge and in-forming (or forming within) the people who read it. In the process, it may be a little wild, but "words ought to be a little wild," said John Maynard Keynes, "for they are an assault of thought upon the unthinking."

Orwell and Bierce are the literary inspiration for this project, but my wife Barb and my sons John and Paul are the personal inspiration. Born in 1979 and 1982, John and Paul will live most of their lives in the next century, if we are conscientious stewards of this one. Inspiration also came from many friends and students, most notably Linda Clements, Gale Holmlund, Jim Harries, Anne Jacobson, and Nancy Evert, who suffered (literally) through my first teaching on this topic, and from JoMarie Williamson, who suffered (again literally) through the preparation of this manuscript. Information, as well as inspiration, came from the librarians at St. Olaf College and the Minneapolis Public Library. And much-needed financial support came from generous grants of St. Olaf College.

My colleagues, both at St. Olaf and elsewhere, have taught me by word and example the
liberating character of liberal arts education,
which insists, as did Thomas Jefferson, that people should be educated "so much as may enable them
to read and understand what is going on in the
world, and to keep their part of it going on
right: for nothing can keep it right but their own
vigilant and distrustful superintendence."

Among the vigilant and distrustful superin-
tendents of the fate of the earth are the nation's
editorial cartoonists. I am honored and thankful
to share the pages of this book with artists who
daily depict the gaps between rhetoric and reality
in our national and international life. Their
work both illustrates and inspires mine, proving,
as I hope that this dictionary does, that the pen
and the pun are as mighty as the sword.

But the original lexical inspiration came
from my father, who always insisted that "English
is a precise language." This book is also dedicated to him. May he rest in peace. May we all
rest in peace.

James J. Farrell
August 6, 1985

A. The first letter of the atomic alphabet; it stands for "atom," as in the quaint Puritan couplet: "In Atom's fall/ We sinned all."

ABM (ANTI-BALLISTIC MISSILE). Intercontinental trapshooting with crapshooting odds; a sport in which targets spring from traps 8,000 miles away and come within range at 10,000 miles per hour; failure to hit all targets makes us all clay pigeons--or dead ducks.
--syn. active defense, ballistic missile defense.
See BMD, DAMAGE LIMITATION, STAR WARS.

ACCEPTABLE FAILURE RATE. An exceptionable euphemism for the 20 million American deaths that civil defense planners consider "acceptable" in a nuclear war.
See CIVIL DEFENSE, UNACCEPTABLE DAMAGE.

ACCIDENTAL WAR. A war in which the nuclear weapons that have been developed and deployed since 1945 inadvertently accomplish what they are designed to do. As Leon Wieseltier says, "A balance of terror is now threatened by a balance of error."
See COMPUTER ERROR, FAIL-SAFE, POSITIVE CONTROL.

ACRONYM. A word composed of letters that spell something but mean nothing; a set of initials but no conclusions; a grammatical shorthand that shortcircuits the brain.
See ABM, MAD, MIRV, NATO, SALT, START, etc.

AIR BURST. An aerial entry to Erebus; an above-ground nuclear explosion designed to maximize heat and blast effects, but minimize fallout. A 20-megaton ground burst excavates a crater 300 to 600 feet deep and a mile wide; an air burst doubles the area of destruction, but carves no crater.

ANTINUKE. A pacifist ABM system designed to shoot down nuclear weapons, not after they get in the air, but before they get off the ground.
See NUCLEAR PACIFIST, PACIFISTS, PEACE, PEACE-KEEPER, PEACEMAKER.

APATHY. Individual isolationism; the indifference that makes the difference in democratic decisions about nuclear weapons.
See CITIZENS, DEFENSE MECHANISM, DEMOCRACY, MAD, REPRESSION, SANE, SCHIZOPHRENIA.

--from <u>Jules Feiffer's America</u> (Random House, 1982).

APPEASEMENT. 1. The 1930s process of pacifying Hitler by permitting the annexation of the Rhineland, Austria, and Czechoslovakia to achieve "peace in our time;" 2. By extension, any negotiations in which the enemy's interests are negotiable; and 3. Any program for peace at any time.
See MUNICH.

APOCALYPSE. The eclipse of population by the apotheosis of nuclear weapons.
See ECOCIDE.

AREA BOMBING. Geographic euphemism for a demographic fact: saturation bombing slaughters thousands of innocent civilians. Area bombing began before World War II; during the war, the firebombing of cities such as Hamburg (42,000 dead) and Dresden (250,000 to 400,000 killed or wounded in one night) set the stage for Hiroshima and Nagasaki.
--syn. saturation bombing, terror bombing.
--ant. precision bombing.
See COUNTERVALUE, GUERNICA.

ARMAGEDDON CHAMBERS. Subterranean hellholes in which the Defense Nuclear Agency simulates "the nuclear environment" to test the survivability of the American war machine. Aurora, for example, is an Armageddon chamber located in White Oak, Maryland, which irradiates weapons with 10 million volts of gamma rays to see if machines survive "enhanced radiation" better than people do.
See DEFENSE NUCLEAR AGENCY, ENHANCED RADIATION WEAPON, NUCLEAR WARFIGHTING.

ARMS. From the root that means "to join or fit together," arms are weapons that blow us apart or keep us apart. Nuclear arms are specialized extensions of human arms, but they are not as versatile, because, as the placard says, "You can't hug your baby with nuclear arms."
See ARMS CONTROL.

ARMS CONTROL. Semantic substitution for the obsolete "disarmament," suggesting that we can <u>control</u> our weapons without destroying them. Arms control agreements generally control obsolete weapons systems, while permitting the uncontrolled proliferation of new and more dangerous systems. They usually ignore the dictum of retired Admiral Noel Gayler, who said that "the way to get rid of nuclear weapons is to get rid of nuclear weapons." See DISARMAMENT, GENERAL AND COMPLETE DISARMAMENT, SALT, START, UNILATERAL DISARMAMENT.

ARMS CONTROL AND DISARMAMENT AGENCY (ACDA). An institutional eunuch established in 1961 to emasculate critics of the arms race just as the United States began its unprecedented build-up of nuclear weapons. The ACDA speaks for arms control in the government, but with its minuscule budget and hawkish directors, it speaks softly without a big stick. One ACDA director, Kenneth Adelman, echoed many of his predecessors when he said, "My policy would be to [conduct arms negotiations] for political reasons. But I think it's a sham." See ARMS CONTROL.

ARMS RACE. A contest of two or more nations to contrive more and better ways of killing people; a race without winners, but not without losers; the race to the finish--literally.
--ant. human race.
See BALANCE OF TERROR.

ATOM. The smallest form of a chemical element, from the Greek word for "indivisible". The division of the indivisible accounts for the wider divisions of the "atomic" age.
See COLD WAR, FISSION, FUSION, SCHIZOPHRENIA.

RACE

--from <u>Herblock Through the Looking Glass</u> (W.W. Norton, 1984).

ATOMIC BOMB. "The atomic bomb," says Phyllis Schlafly, "is a marvelous gift that was given to our country by a wise God." Ms. Schlafly, who is Right on so many things, does not explain who gave it to everybody else.
See HYDROGEN BOMB.

ATOMIC ENERGY COMMISSION. The American board charged with the domestic control of atomic energy from 1946 to 1974. The "atomic secret" was committed to the AEC in 1946, and they have since committed it to the commination of foreign nations, the commissions and profits of U.S. businesses, and the electrification of the American people. The AEC's "control" of atomic energy included both promotion and regulation; the AEC generally interpreted these functions as successive steps, until 1974, when it was divided into a promotional agency (ERDA) and the Nuclear Regulatory Agency.
See ATOMS FOR PEACE.

ATOMS FOR PEACE. The silver lining in the mushroom cloud; an American program to use atomic energy to produce electricity, among other things. Since 1953, the program has produced about 80 nuclear reactors, each of which is a prime target in a nuclear war; an enrichment program to produce fissionable uranium, plutonium, deuterium, and tritium, all of which are bomb-grade material; a multi-billion dollar industry that would collapse without government subsidy and insurance; and kilotons of waste that remains radioactive and lethal for thousands of years.
See LOCA, MELTDOWN, REACTOR, THREE MILE ISLAND, WASTE.

ATTRIT. Attrition so abbreviated that it means
death, as in calculations of "attrits per second"
in a nuclear war.
See MEGADEATH.

AUTOMATICISM. The tripwire technique by which Americans stationed in Europe are invited to trip the
fight fantastic with Soviet soldiers.
See STRATEGIC COUPLING.

B-1. The Pentagon's paragon of planned obsolescence;
a strategic bomber intended to replace the B-52
and to be replaced by the Stealth bomber in the
1990s. The original price of the B-1 was $20 mil-
lion; when President Jimmy Carter canceled the B-1
in favor of cruise missiles in 1977, the price was
$90 million; in the Reagan reincarnation of this
"wealth" bomber, the price reached $553 million
each. If the plane accelerated as fast as the
price rises, it might be worth it.
See BUY-IN, STEALTH.

BACKFIRE. The new Soviet intermediate-range bomber
which--with the American cruise missile--backfired
the SALT II talks for several years, because the
U.S. considered it a strategic bomber and the USSR
did not.
See MEDIUM BOMBER.

BALANCE. A journalistic convention that journalists
must present "both sides" of an issue without
determining if either is true. The truth, it is
assumed, "lies" somewhere in the middle.
See NEWSPEAK.

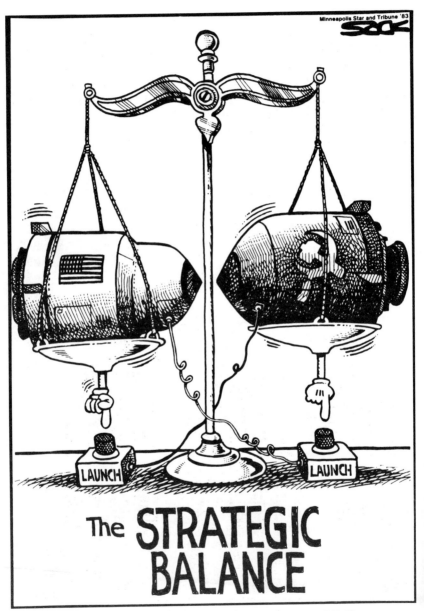

Reprinted with permission from the Minneapolis Star and Tribune.

BALANCE OF TERROR. The quintessence of terrorism; the delicate balance of two unequal forces, each of which claims to have less effective and survivable throw-weight than the other. The beauty of this term is that it focuses attention on the balance and the terror rather than on the increasing overkill capability of both sides.
--syn. strategic balance.
See DETERRENCE, OVERKILL, STABLE DETERRENCE.

BARGAINING CHIPS. New weapons that we won't deploy if they scrap already existing weapons. "Reducing something now, in exchange for something that might come along later, is a perfectly fair bargain," observed ACDA director Eugene Rostow. Thus, bargaining chips are new weapons that we will justifiably develop and deploy, as we did with MIRVs and cruise missiles.
See BLACKMAIL, CREDULOUS.

Reprinted with permission from the Minneapolis Star and Tribune.

BETTER RED THAN DEAD. The heretical slogan that suggests that losing a war would be preferable to losing the primary reason for a war--our lives. One-hundred-percent Americans agree instead with Senator Richard Russell, chairman of the Armed Services Committee, who felt that "if we have to start all over again with Adam and Eve, then I want them to be Americans and not Russians, and I want them on this continent and not on Europe."
See UN-AMERICAN.

BIAS. The bent of missiles to miss, which dismisses the certainty of experts bent on first-strike capability; a mathematical measure, like circular error probable, representing the distance between the center of a cluster of impact points and the intended target, as established by test results, which are themselves misleading, since they occur on an East-West trajectory, instead of the North-South polar route of real missiles. Besides gravitational and electromagnetic idiosyncrasies, bias can result from faulty programming, hardware defects, or weather conditions at the point of re-entry. The result is that the only thing we know for sure is that we're not sure how accurate our missiles will be in a real-death situation.
See CIRCULAR ERROR PROBABLE, FIRST STRIKE, PRE-EMPTIVE STRIKE.

BIKINI. A two-piece word, denoting both the beach site for atomic bomb testing and the beach sight of anatomic bombshells.
See TESTING.

BISHOPS. Spiritual shepherds who have begun to speak
their peace about nuclear weapons. Their 1983
pastoral letter tries to keep their American flock
from being fleeced by the Russian bear, or by the
cry of "Wolf!" from an administration of hawks in
sheeps' clothing.
See IDEALISM.

Reprinted by permission of United Feature Syndicate, Inc.

BLACK BRIEFCASE. The coffer whose use precedes cof-
fins for us all; the briefing for a descent into
hell; the attacké case that contains the Emergency
War Order (EWO) codes by which the President can
authorize a nuclear war.
--syn. football.
See C3I, MAJOR ATTACK OPTION, SIOP.

BLACKMAIL. Enemy bargaining chips.
See BARGAINING CHIPS.

BLAST WAVE. A breaker on the shores of eternity, a tidal wave of air pressure and winds that undulates from the center of an explosion, inundating people and property beneath a stream of destruction. One mile away from a one-megaton air burst, overpressure reaches 43 psi and winds reach 1700 mph. Ten miles away, the overpressure drops to 4 psi (still enough to smash homes) and winds dwindle to a mere 130 mph, making ballistic missiles of human beings who made and paid for ballistic missiles.
--syn. shock wave, wave goodbye.
See FIREBALL, FIRESTORM, RADIATION SICKNESS, SHOCK WAVE.

BLEEDING HEART LIBERAL. A person whose figurative heartbleed may prevent the literal heartbleed and heartbreak that would result from a nuclear war.
See CITIZENS, DEMOCRACY.

BMD. Ballistic Missile Defense; systems that defend against ballistic missiles, but attack strategic stability and deterrence.
See ABM, STAR WARS.

THE BOMB. A synechdoche that reduces 50,000 nuclear weapons to a lone danger, a capital(ized) expression of our capitulation to capital punishment.
See THE BUTTON.

BOMBER GAP. The gap between the ears of those who thought the missile gap of 1960 was a new idea. The bomber gap allegedly opened in 1954-55 when the Soviet Union began to produce Bear and Bison intermediate range bombers, and it lasted until Sputnik opened the missile gap in 1957.
See MISSILE GAP, WINDOW OF VULNERABILITY.

BOY. 1. A male child; 2. A successful nuclear explosion. "The women's liberation movement will never forgive me for my telegram to Los Alamos when I learned of the first successful H-bomb test in the Pacific," says Edward Teller, father of the H-bomb. "The full text was 'It's a boy.'"
See LITTLE BOY.

BREEDER. A reactor that breeds trouble by producing more fissionable material--especially plutonium--than it consumes.
See PLUTONIUM, REACTOR.

BROKEN ARROW. Smoke screen for a barbed shaft; code name for an accident involving nuclear weapons or warheads.
See ACCIDENTAL WAR, FAIL-SAFE.

BUILD-DOWN. 1. The "less is more" of strategic architecture; a process of deploying more modern warheads without deploying more warheads, specifically an arms control proposal to decommission two warheads for each new one deployed; this proposal is sometimes called "two-for-one" because it allows Congress to tell its opposing constituents both "I am for reducing nuclear weapons" and "I support modernizing our arsenal;" 2. A process of superhardening subterranean missile silos to withstand the blast effects of the new counterforce weapons deployed in the build-down; 3. A process of employing oxymoronic neologisms to shroud the destabilizing tendencies of smaller nuclear forces with higher counterforce concentrations.
--syn. build-up, trade-up.
--ant. disarmament.
See ARMS CONTROL, DISARMAMENT, MODERNIZATION, SALT, START.

THE BUTTON. Minuscule metaphor for the decision that would touch off a touch-and-go world.

Dana Summers. The Orlando Sentinel. Reprinted with permission.

BUY-IN. A misleading cost estimate designed to get a government contract; after the contract is secured, it's good-bye to the good buy.
See B-1, MILITARY-INDUSTRIAL-COMPLEX, PROFIT.

C3I. Command, control, communication, and intelligence ("see-cubed-eye"); the seeing-eye god of the military; systems of detection, assessment and response to actual or potential military conflict.
See EMP.

CALCULATED RISK. A ruse for a risk that means, according to James Thurber, "We have every hope and assurance that the plan will be successful, but if it doesn't work we knew all the time it wouldn't and said so."
See ACCEPTABLE FAILURE RATE, EXPERT, FAIL-SAFE.

CHAIN REACTION. The great divide of nuclear physics, in which sustained atomic scission occurs, linking science to the schemes of nuclear power generation and the schism of the Cold War.
See FISSION, REACTOR.

CHINA SYNDROME. 1. First Lady Nancy Reagan's affinity for tableware that cost $209,000; 2. A possible consequence of a reactor fuel meltdown, namely that the molten fuel drops through the floor of the reactor and into the earth; 3. The delusion of diplomats that China will tip the balance of power in their favor.
See MELTDOWN.

CIRCULAR ERROR PROBABLE (CEP). A measure of missile accuracy, CEP is the radius of the circle around a target in which 50 percent of the warheads will fall. The CEP for Pershing II, for the cruise missile, and for the Trident II is a matter of feet. Said Senator Barry Goldwater of the cruise missile, "We could lob one right into the men's room of the Kremlin."
See COUNTERFORCE, DESTABILIZING WEAPONS, LETHALITY, TERCOM.

CITIZENS. We, the people, who sit passively while our elected representatives spend our money to insure that government of the people, by the people, and for the people shall perish with the earth; also spelled "sitizen." Rabbi Abraham Joshua Heschel reminds such citizens that "in a free society some may be guilty, but all are responsible."
--syn. passivist.
--ant. pacifist.
See DEMOCRACY, TAXES.

CIVIL DEFENSE. Uncivil and indefensible program of post-preventive detention whereby citizens hide in shelters and/or rural areas from the consequences of their inaction.
--syn. passive defense.
See CRISIS RELOCATION, FALLOUT SHELTER, FEMA.

CIVIL DEFENSE SIREN. A guided whistle that conditions non-combatants to accept their roles as hostages and victims of the nuclear age. Named for the figures of Greek mythology who lured sailors to their death on the rocky coast.
See CIVIL DEFENSE, STRATEGIC WARNING.

CIVIL DISOBEDIENCE. A truly civil defense; the peace de resistance of nuclear protest; a method of upholding the law of God by withholding support from the contrary laws of men.
See PACIFISTS, TAX RESISTANCE.

CLEAN BOMB. An enhanced radiation weapon which cleans the landscape of life, but litters it with corpses, OR a fusion bomb with very little fission and, therefore, relatively little fallout.
See ENHANCED RADIATION WEAPON, NEUTRON BOMB, REDUCED RESIDUAL RADIATION WEAPON.

COFFIN. 1. A cask in which radioactive material is transported; 2. The casket in which most victims of nuclear war will not be buried, because the demand will exceed the supply. Instead, FEMA has considered supplying shelters with body bags, the number depending on the number of shelter occupants and the calculated 30-day death rate in the post-exchange recovery sceneario.
See FEMA, MEGADEATH, POST-EXCHANGE RECOVERY SCENARIO.

PICNIC

--from Herblock Through the Looking Glass (W.W. Norton, 1984).

COLD WAR. The polar turbulence located between the US and the USSR which controls world whether--whether or not there will still be a world tomorrow. This cold front of World War II developed over Eastern Europe, but now affects the entire international atmosphere. Its storm systems are economic, ideological, and military; the temperate characteristics of the military storm are maintained by strategic brainstorming that avoids precipitous action because of the mutually assured destruction of deterrence and proxy wars like Korea, Vietnam, and Central America.

The coldness of the Cold War confuses even military meteorologists. The colder it gets, the closer it approaches the boiling point. And a thaw seems to reduce the forecast of hot war. The hotness of hot war is, however, unequivocable; the temperature of a nuclear fireball reaches several million degrees Fahrenheit.
See CONTAINMENT.

COLLATERAL DAMAGE. Euphemism for the incidental mass murder of innocent civilians, specifically those people killed and property damaged in a counterforce attack. Depending on the type of attack and sheltering preparations, a U.S. counterforce attack on the USSR would cause collateral damage of 3.7 million to 27.7 million lives.
--syn. bonus.
See COUNTERFORCE.

COMBAT CASUALTY PREDICTION CODE. A measure of the nuclear warfighting capability of human beings, with which the Armed Forces Radiobiology Research Institute estimates the effects of radiation exposure on the "combat effectiveness" of American

soldiers. The code shows, for example, that tank loaders exposed to 1000 rads of radiation would remain "combat effective" for about 100 minutes; nausea, vomiting, and fatigue would render them "combat ineffective" within a day, and they would die within a month.
See DEFENSE NUCLEAR AGENCY, NUCLEAR WARFIGHTING, PRIMATE EQUILIBRIUM PLATFORM.

COMMITTEE ON THE PRESENT DANGER. A group founded in 1976 by Eugene Rostow and Paul Nitze which believes that the present danger can be overcome by greater future danger. According to Robert Scheer, the Committee claimed "that the Soviets were in the process of attaining superiority in nuclear and conventional weapons; that they were bent on world conquest; that the United States, misled by the spirit of detente, had disarmed during the seventies while the Soviets went barreling ahead in the arms race; that nuclear deterrence and the assumption of Mutual Assured Destruction were no longer adequate; and that the Soviets were in fact preparing to fight and win a nuclear war." Consequently, they opposed SALT II and proposed an unprecedented build-up of American arms. Ronald Reagan made the Committee a present danger by making its members officials, including Eugene Rostow, director of the Arms Control and Disarmament Agency; Paul Nitze, Theater Nuclear Forces negotiatior in Geneva; George Schultz, Secretary of State; Richard Allen, National Security advisor; Jeane Kirkpatrick, Ambassador to the United Nations; William Casey, director of the CIA; Fred Ikle, Undersecretary of Defense for Policy; and Richard Perle, Assistant Secretary of Defense for International Security Policy.
See REAGAN(AT)OMICS.

COMMON SENSE. The uncommon intelligence of people like Thomas Powers, who notes that "since 1945, the United States and the Soviet Union have been preparing to fight each other in a big war, and eventually they are going to do it. This is a bleak prospect, but I can't think of a way we might escape it--that is, a realistic way, one we might really adopt. We may want things to turn out differently, but wanting is not enough. Everything we have <u>done</u> is consistent with preparation for war. When the war comes, we shall fight it with the weapons at hand, and those prominently include nuclear weapons."
--ant. expertise.
See EXPERT, THINK TANK.

COMPREHENSIVE TEST BAN. A proposed international agreement to put an end to atomic testing before the tests (and their upshot) put an end to us. Every American President from John Kennedy to Jimmy Carter supported a comprehensive test ban. But Ronald Reagan suspended negotiations in July 1982 because of alleged problems of verification, and because he wants the United States to develop and deploy a generation of destabilizing weapons.
See DESTABILIZING WEAPONS, LIMITED TEST BAN, MODERNIZATION, TESTING, VERIFICATION.

COMPUTER ERROR. A nuclear blunder-buss that could massacre millions; a thinkable cause of the unthinkable. In 1982, Senator Mark Hatfield testified before the Foreign Relations Committee that "during the past 20 months US computer malfunction has falsely signaled a Soviet strategic attack 147 times." In 1980, Senators Barry Goldwater and Gary Hart found 151 false alarms in 18 months.
See ACCIDENTAL WAR, FAIL-SAFE, LAUNCH ON WARNING.

CONFIDENCE-BUILDING MEASURES. Treaties and agreements that promote the exchange of information that could prevent the exchange of nuclear weapons, e.g., the hotline, the Standing Consultative Commission, and shared information on weapons inventories.
See HOTLINE.

CONFLICT SPECTRUM. A continuum of contention, from threats to third strikes. When, in 1982, National Security Advisor William Clark referred to "the high end of the conflict spectrum," he meant, in a word, war.
See EUPHEMISM.

CONTAINMENT. The American policy of preventing the expansion of Soviet influence in the world by extending American influence to the borders of the USSR. The policy is implemented with strategic nuclear weapons, military alliances, and American military bases overseas.
See DOMINO THEORY.

CONTROL RODS. Cadmium wands that constrain the wanderlust of neutrons in a nuclear reactor, thus allowing a sustained chain reaction.
See CHAIN REACTION, NUCLEAR REACTOR.

CONVENTIONAL WEAPONS. 1. Nonnuclear weapons that are more homicidal than genocidal; 2. Weapons sanctioned by custom or usage, like the weapons of World War II, which killed 52 million people. As soon as nuclear weapons are widely used, they will become "conventional."
--syn. general purpose forces.
--ant. nuclear weapons.
See STRATEGIC WEAPONS, TACTICAL NUCLEAR WEAPONS.

CONVERSION. 1. A spiritual transformation or rebirth; 2. Beating swords into plowshares, the shift from "Peace Through Strength" to "Strength Through Peace."
See JUSTICE, PEACE THROUGH STRENGTH, SANE.

CORE DISRUPTIVE ACCIDENT. The rapid release of uncontrolled energy in a nuclear reactor; an explosion.
See ENERGETIC DISASSEMBLY, MELTDOWN, MURPHY'S LAW, NORMAL ABERRATION, THREE MILE ISLAND.

COST-BENEFIT ANALYSIS. A type of reasoning that asks how many people perish per penny. The cost refers to the money; the benefit refers to the corpses.
See EXPERT, THINK TANK.

COUNTERFORCE. Offensive strategy with a defensive sound, specifically the targeting of the enemy's missiles, bombers, and military installations. Designed to destroy these weapons and command posts before their attack, counterforce weapons appear in scenarios for a pre-emptive first strike or protracted nuclear war. Counterforce calms the moral qualms of those who oppose the indiscriminate killing of innocent people in countervalue targeting, but it does not calm the qualms of the enemy, who interprets counterforce capability as evidence of offensive intentions. Nor does it save the innocent civilians, since they may die as collateral damage in a counterforce strike. But counterforce does provide a rationale for the arms race, since both sides need counterforce weapons to target the other side's counterforce weapons, which threaten the survivability of the retaliatory strike that makes deterrence "work."

"Discriminate aiming [or counterforce targeting] in a nuclear war is logically and morally equivalent to using a sledgehammer to kill a fly on someone's head," says Robert Gardiner. "It is surely possible to kill a fly in this manner; but we must ask: Is it also possible, by any stretch of the imagination, to claim that the ensuing death of the person was only incidental to the death of the fly, or that smashing of the skull was not intended in the intention of the act?"
--syn. dynamic deterrence, pre-emptive deterrence.
See CIRCULAR ERROR PROBABLE, COLLATERAL DAMAGE, COUNTERVALUE, DETERRENCE, DOUBLE EFFECT, FIRST STRIKE, NUCLEAR WARFIGHTING.

COUNTERVALUE. 1. The strategic foundation of deterrence, specifically missiles targeted to destroy enemy cities, civilians, and civilization. Reliance on countervalue deterrence (or massive retaliation) led a 1960s Pentagon analyst to the conclusion that "weapons that kill people are more peace-loving than weapons that kill weapons"; 2. Opposed to values; immoral; unethical. Vatican II, for example, declared that "any act of war aimed indiscriminately at the destruction of entire cities or of extensive areas along with the population is a crime against God and man himself. It merits unequivocal and unhesitating condemnation."
--syn. city-busting, countercity, demographic targeting.
--ant. counterforce.
See AREA BOMBING, BALANCE OF TERROR, COUNTERFORCE, DETERRENCE, GENOCIDE, GUERNICA, MAD, UNACCEPTABLE DAMAGE.

COUNTERVAILING STRATEGY. The empire's new clothes for flexible response, countervailing strategy was an unavailing 1980 political strategy of President Jimmy Carter, promising conventional or counterforce capability to match any level of Soviet strike.
See FLEXIBLE RESPONSE, FLEXIBLE TARGETING.

CREDIBILITY. 1. The ability to convince the enemy, the allies, and the public that your lies are true; 2. "In safeguards," according to the government's Safeguards Dictionary, "the capability to satisfy the public that safeguards are effective." A credible deterrent, notes William Safire, is "a defense that needn't be effective as long as the enemy thinks it is."
See PROPAGANDA, SAFEGUARDS.

CREDULOUS. The state or condition of Congressmen or citizens who believe that MX missiles (or any other bargaining chip) will help the President achieve a new arms control agreement.
See BARGAINING CHIPS, MX, SCOWCROFT COMMISSION.

CRISIS RELOCATION. Instant urban renewal; a wreakend trip to the country; euphemism for evacuation of the cities preceding nuclear war. As people move from "risk" to "host" areas, the crisis is relocated in two ways: 1) the leaders who caused the crisis shift the burden to their people, and 2) the crisis of the cities becomes a crisis of the countryside. Minor problem: this plan requires 3 to 8 days notice, but ICBMs arrive in 30 minutes, and they will relocate urban populations even more effectively than the Office of Civil Defense.
See CIVIL DEFENSE, FEMA.

CRISIS STABILITY. An oxymoron denoting the aplomb with which nations greet a crisis when their strategic forces are impervious to preemption. First-strike weapons threaten crisis stability with use-them-or-lose-them options.
See DESTABILIZING WEAPONS, LAUNCH-ON-WARNING, PRE-EMPTVE STRIKE, SURVIVABILITY, VULNERABILITY.

CRITICAL MASS. 1. The smallest amount of fissionable material that can sustain a chain reaction; 2. The number of critical citizens needed to restrain the chain reaction of the arms race.
--syn. significant quantity.
See CHAIN REACTION, CITIZENS.

CROSS TARGETING. A doublecrossed double negative; to insure the negation of a target, two warheads from two separate missiles are aimed at one target.
See LETHALITY, OVERKILL, REDUNDANCY.

CRUISE MISSILE. A nuclear "Love Boat," this drone cruises through the atmosphere at subsonic speeds and low altitude, thus evading enemy radar, to deliver its one celebrity passenger within a few hundred feet of its point of deathly debarcation.
See DESTABILIZING WEAPONS.

DAMAGE LIMITATION. A genus of wishful thinking, four species of which are ABM, air defense, civil defense, and counterforce targeting. Damage limitation is a strategy, largely rhetorical, for snatching victory out of the jaws of deceit. It is essential to both warfighting and warwinning strategies, but those who employ the term, said former Secretary of State Dean Rusk, are "playing with words unrelated to the real world."
See ABM, CIVIL DEFENSE, COUNTERFORCE, WIN.

DECAPITATION. The beheading of a government by the destruction of its leadership with strategic nuclear weapons. The main flaw of this capitol punishment is that it kills the commanders who could commute the executioner's death sentence.
See COUNTERFORCE.

DEFENSE MECHANISM. The most popular defense in the nuclear age; a psychological behavior that conceals anxiety from people, based on the unconscious belief that out of fright is out of mind.
See APATHY, FATALIST, REPRESSION, SANE, SCHIZOPHRENIA.

DEFENSE NUCLEAR AGENCY (DNA). The Senseless Bureau which practices "the art of testing nuclear weapons effects phenomenology," analyzing how men and machines perform in what is quaintly called "the nuclear environment." Appropriately, DNA's logo is three arrows bracketed by mushroom clouds.
See ARMAGEDDON CHAMBERS, COMBAT CASUALTY PREDICTION CODE, PRIMATE EQUILIBRIUM PLATFORM.

DEGRADATION. 1. The degraded circumlocution for the collapse of command, control, communication, and intelligence in a nuclear war. U.S. war planners hope that American C3I will "degrade gracefully," so that we can degrade the Soviet Union less gracefully; 2. The process by which military upgrading degrades our social and moral life.
See C3I, DECAPITATION.

DELIVERY SYSTEM. An intercontinental parcel post, with recipients cashed in on delivery; specifically, any means (ballistic missiles, cruise missiles, bombers) of delivering nuclear warheads.
See NUCLEAR EXCHANGE.

DEMOCRACY. That system of government of, buy, and form the people by which citizens elect representatives who vote to create an atomic autocracy which uses classification and clearance systems to conceal nuclear policy from the citizens.
See ATOMIC ENERGY COMMISSION, CITIZENS.

DENSE PACK. 1. The pack of lies and untested assumptions that supported MX deployment in clusters of superhardened missile silos, specifically the assumptions that incoming Soviet warheads would commit fratricide, that the MX missiles would not be harmed by such explosions, and that the Soviets wouldn't use time-delay weapons or bigger bombs; 2. The basing system itself, to wit, about 100 missiles in a 10 to 15 square mile area.
--syn. closely spaced basing.
See FRATRICIDE, MX.

DEPARTMENT OF DEFENSE. Cabinet agency charged with the defense of the indefensible; new name (1947) for the Department of War; likely inspiration for Orwell's Ministry of Peace. Unfortunately, defense is one thing this department does not provide, because there is no effective defense against ballistic missiles, and because, as Lewis Mumford said, "There is no defense against genocide by countergenocide."
See PENTAGON.

DESTABILIZING WEAPONS. Those weapons that, because of accuracy and speed, tempt nations to first-strike options or launch-on-warning responses. Among the destabilizing weapons the United States plans to deploy in the 1980s are the MX missile, Trident II, and Pershing II.
See CIRCULAR ERROR PROBABLE, COUNTERFORCE, FIRST STRIKE, LAUNCH ON WARNING.

DETENTE. An interval of reduced tensions in the Cold War (1972-1979) in which the Soviet Union added 5,000 warheads, 3 new land based missiles, a new submarine, new submarine-launched missile systems and MIRVed missiles to its arsenal, and the United States, not to be outdone in its expressions of amity, added the Trident submarine, the Trident missile system, the long-range cruise missile, and 5,500 new warheads, many on MIRVed missiles.

As "news-speak," detente "meets all the requirements," notes journalist Paul Braaten. "It is French, and therefore impossible to pronounce with any degree of certainty; it is short enough to fit in a one-column headline, should that unfortunate necessity arise, yet full-bodied enough to add solidity and a sense of importance to a four column head-cum-kicker; its meaning is only hazily grasped by its users, and, perhaps most important of all, it means nothing whatever to the reader." See ARMS CONTROL, SALT, SOVIET THREAT.

AUTH

Detente

Tony Auth. The Philadelphia Inquirer. Reprinted with permission.

DETERRENCE. The international version of winning through intimidation; the policy of preventing enemy attack by threatening the same; preserving peace by preparing for death; a mutual genocide pact to prevent aggression.
See BALANCE OF TERROR, DOOMSDAY DEVICE, GRADUATED DETERRENCE, INTRAWAR DETERRENCE, MAD, MINIMUM DETERRENCE.

DEVICE. 1. A linguistic contrivance that divests the word "bomb" of its invidious overtones; 2. A nuclear bomb.
See BOY.

34

DIRT. The pall for people passing from asses to ashes in the shoveled shelters of the post-attack recovery scenario.
See CIVIL DEFENSE, POST-ATTACK RECOVERY SCENARIO, SHOVEL.

DISARMAMENT. The process of negotiation and agreement about levels of nuclear armament, so called because such talks disarm critics of the arms race. For example, an article on the start of START talks noted that "the very fact that the superpowers are talking directly gives Western governments some relief from the ferment that has been building publicly over nuclear armaments." Some literalists have interpreted this word to mean the reduction of weapons or delivery systems; to prevent such unwarranted confusion, the preferred term is now "arms control."
See ARMS CONTROL, SALT, START, UNILATERAL DISARMAMENT.

Oliphant by Pat Oliphant. (c) 1977. United Press Syndicate.
Reprinted with permission. All rights reserved.

DIVERSION. 1. The redirection of nuclear material from lawful to unlawful purposes, by the authorities or by theft; 2. A diversionary tactic--like TV, sports, cars, fast food, or spending--that keeps the public's attention focused on private affairs instead of the public business.
See SAFEGUARDS.

DOMINO THEORY. A 1954 analysis of international relations by President Eisenhower, who observed that "you have a row of dominoes set up, and you knock over the first one, and what would happen to the last one is the certainty that it would go over quickly. So you have a beginning of a disintegration that would have the most profound influences." With his characteristic simplemindedness, President Reagan stated the maxim more clearly: "Let's not delude ourselves; the Soviet Union underlies all the unrest in the world that's going on. If they weren't engaged in this game of dominoes, there wouldn't be any hot spots in the world."

Unfortunately, in the game of dominoes, you <u>don't</u> have a row of dominoes set up, nor do you knock them over. In the international analogy, if you have a row of dominoes set up, you should ask who set them up, and why they are spaced so closely. In the instance of Vietnam, French colonialism set up the dominoes, and nationalism knocked them down. In Central America, injustice and exploitation set them up, and hope is knocking them down. But dominoes is in fact a game of matching, in which you have to match the opponent to win. If

the opponent has popular and political support, you must match it with popular and political moves. In such a situation, military moves lead only to the boneyard.
See CONTAINMENT.

Reprinted with permission of the Minneapolis Star and Tribune.

DOOMSDAY. Today and tomorrow.

DOOMSDAY CLOCK. The clock on the front cover of the <u>Bulletin</u> <u>of the Atomic Scientists</u> which tells the time of our lives. Set first at 7 minutes before midnight in 1947, it has been as close as 2 minutes from 1953 to 1963, and as far as 12 minutes in 1963 and 1972. It stands now at 3 minutes to midnight.

DOOMSDAY DEVICE. 1. An imaginary machine wired to destroy the earth in case of enemy attack; 2. Deterrence; 3. Faustian man.
See COMPUTER ERROR, ECOCIDE, LAUNCH ON WARNING, MAD, NUCLEAR WINTER.

DOUBLE EFFECT. The doublethink that allows some moralists to justify the collateral damage of a counterforce nuclear attack as a mere part of the dual effect of the bomb on military and civilian elements of the society.

In their May 1983 pastoral letter, the Roman Catholic bishops of the United States commented on this notion: "We are told that some weapons are designed for purely 'counterforce' use against military forces and targets. The moral issue, however, is not resolved by the design of weapons or the planned intention for use; there are also consequences which must be assessed. It would be a perverted political policy or moral casuistry which tried to justify a weapon which 'indirectly' or 'unintentionally' killed a million innocent people because they happened to live near a 'militarily significant target.'"
See BISHOPS, COLLATERAL DAMAGE, COUNTERFORCE, DOUBLESPEAK, DOUBLETHINK.

DOUBLESPEAK. The forked tongue of atomic diplomacy, the international language of the nuclear age.
See DOUBLETHINK, EUPHEMISM.

DOUBLETHINK. Hypocoristic hypocrisy; according to Orwell, "the power of holding two contradictory beliefs in one's mind simultaneously, and accepting both of them." "In the doublethink world," claims Haig Bosmajian, "'War is Peace' and an intercontinental weapon devised to kill and destroy is a 'Peacekeeper.' In the doublethink world, 'Freedom is Slavery' and totalitarian countries are part of the Free World. In the doublethink world, 'Ignorance is Strength' and increasing censorship, less access to information, increases strength."
See FREE WORLD, PEACEKEEPER.

DR. STRANGELOVE. The eponymous think-tank Kahn-man of Stanley Kubrick's 1964 movie who only coincidentally resembles Herman Kahn, Henry Kissinger, and Edward Teller, with their implicit message to stop worrying and love the bomb.
See EXPERT, THINK TANK.

DUAL-CAPABLE SYSTEMS. Double trouble for verification and arms control; duel-capable weapons that can be equipped with conventional or nuclear explosives.
See VERIFICATION.

DUPE. Variant spelling of "dope"; an American of one peace with a Russian, specifically a person who can be tricked into thinking that some Soviet propaganda is credible because it is true, and that some Soviet objectives--like bilateral disarmament--coincide with some American objectives.
See UN-AMERICAN.

ECOCIDE. The -cide-show of the nuclear circus, in which Midgetman and other atomic mutations side with the distinct possibility that one side effect of nuclear war is the extinction of the first, and perhaps the only, evolution of life on earth.
See MIDGETMAN, NUCLEAR WINTER.

ELECTROMAGNETIC PULSE (EMP). The EMPeror of iced screams; an electrical embolism in the circulatory system of the body politic, disabling electronic circuits in cars, communication systems, and computers with the electromagnetic effects of a nuclear explosion. The electromagnetic pulse of a single empyrean bomb could incapacitate not only network TV (which some would consider a blessing) but C3I capabilities as well.
See C3I.

Don Wright. The Miami News. Reprinted with permission.

ENCRYPTION. The cryptic name for coding of missile telemetry in order to reduce enemy intelligence-gathering to a cipher. Encryption that interferes with the vital process of verification is forbidden by the unratified Salt II treaty.
See NATIONAL TECHNICAL MEANS, TELEMETRY, VERIFICATION.

ENEMY. 1. An adversary or opponent, an armed foe or opposing military force, a hostile nation or state; in short, "them." 2. A group of mothers, fathers, lovers, lawyers, beggars, sons, bosses, farmers, daughters, and soldiers on the other side who are just as vulnerable as you are.

"Once a nation bases its security on an absolute weapon, such as the atom bomb," observed Patrick Blackett in 1956, "it becomes psychologically necessary to believe in an absolute enemy."
--syn. us.
See SOVIET THREAT.

ENERGETIC DISASSEMBLY. The assuasive neologism for an explosion, produced as a part of the nuclear industry's entitlement program.
See CORE DISRUPTIVE ACCIDENT, MURPHY's LAW, NORMAL ABERRATION.

ENHANCED RADIATION WEAPON. Neutron bomb. The 1977 winner of the Doublespeak Award of the Committee on Public Doublespeak of the National Council of Teachers of English, this enhanced euphemism evades the effects of this new, improved radiation: within hours severe shock sets in, accompanied by vomiting and diarrhea. Victims pass blood because of massive internal damage, then fever sets in. Sometimes recovery seems to occur,

but internal bleeding begins again, hair falls out, and the throat and intestines are covered with ulcers. Bone marrow rots in the living body, and disease-resisting white blood cells are destroyed, leaving the body susceptible to blood poisoning and death from infections as minor as a cold.
--syn. enlarged radiation weapon.
See CLEAN BOMB, NEUTRON BOMB, RADIATION SICKNESS.

Feiffer

Feiffer by Jules Feiffer. (c) 1978. United Press Syndicate.
Reprinted with permission. All rights reserved.

EQUIVALENT MEGATONNAGE. The "Small is Beautiful" measure of destruction that takes into account the fact that small nuclear explosions do <u>proportionately</u> more damage than large ones. Thus, while the Soviet Union has more throwweight and megatonnage than the U.S., the Americans have more warheads and greater equivalent megatonnage.
See MEGATON, THROWWEIGHT.

ESCALATION. The intensified tide of battle; the upward mobility of morbidity in war; the direct approach to eschatology.
See ESCALATION LADDER, INTRAWAR DETERRENCE.

ESCALATION DOMINANCE. The ability, at any level of escalation, to come out on top of the heap. Theoretically, escalation dominance provides intrawar deterrence by demonstrating superiority all the way up the escalation ladder to overkill; more practically, escalation dominance provides a rationale for unlimited weapons procurement.
See ESCALATION LADDER, INTRAWAR DETERRENCE.

ESCALATION LADDER. A stairway to the scars; a hypothetical series of increasingly violent attacks that make nuclear war seem predictable, controllable, and thinkable. Herman Kahn's escalation ladder proceeded from "ostensible crisis" (#1) to "barely nuclear war" (#15) to "local nuclear war--exemplary" (#21) to "reciprocal reprisals" (#31) to "slow-motion counter-'property' war" (#33) to "countervalue salvo" (#40) to "civilian devastation attack" (#42), and ended with "spasm or insensate war" (#44).
See FLEXIBLE RESPONSE, INTRAWAR DETERRENCE, NUCLEAR WARFIGHTING.

ETERNITY. The never-never land of strategists and people who think that we will <u>never</u> use the nuclear weapons we have.
See MURPHY'S LAW.

EUPHEMISM. Phony euphony; a delicate rhetorical expression designed to please the senses without making sense; telling it like it isn't.
See DOUBLESPEAK, DOUBLETHINK.

EXCHANGE RATIO. The quid pro quotient of the number of friendly warheads raised to the number of enemy warheads razed in a counterforce attack. The MX missile provides the Soviet Union with a favorable exchange ratio, because it takes only 2 of their warheads to destroy 10 of ours.
See MIDGETMAN, MX, POST-EXCHANGE RATIOS.

EXPERT. 1. A person who believes in the power of positivist thinking, and knows how to win fiends and influence people; 2. A ratiocinerator who could say, as did U.S. Defense Department consultant Colin Gray, "The United States must possess the ability to wage nuclear war rationally."

John Trever. The Albuquerque Journal. Reprinted with permission.

EXTREMISTS. Persons or politicians, both Democratic and Republican, who accept the orthodox view that "Exterminism in the defense of liberty is no vice."
See DETERRENCE, GENOCIDE.

FAIL-SAFE. A set of command-and-control procedures and mechanisms designed by fallible human beings to protect them from the consequences of their fallibility; specifically a set of two commands for bombers: the first authorizes take-off, the second verifies the command to strike. If bombers in the air <u>fail</u> to receive the second command, they return <u>safely</u> to base.
See ACCIDENTAL WAR, NORMAL ABERRATION, NUCLEAR SAFEGUARDS, POSITIVE CONTROL.

FALLOUT. Crop dusting for people; radioactive particles of people and places raised by a ground burst that "fall in" to cities, suburbs, farms, lakes and streams. The more experienced Japanese call fallout "ashes of death."
See GROUND BURST, RADIATION SICKNESS.

FALLOUT SHELTER. An advanced form of pre-need funeral planning, in which people inter themselves to wait for death, which will come sooner, in the form of blast and thermal effects; later, in asphyxiation caused as the firestorm sucks oxygen out of the crypt; or ultimately, in starvation, as nuclear winter and fallout kill crops and contaminate cropland. A mausoleum for the living dead.
--syn. bomb shelter.
See CIVIL DEFENSE, DAMAGE LIMITATION, FALLOUT, FIRESTORM, NUCLEAR WINTER.

FATALIST. A psychological casualty of immanent nuclear war, a person who submits--without protest--to the fate of living in expectation of imminent extinction.
See APATHY, PSYCHIC NUMBING.

FEAR. The scare tissue of the nuclear wound, cause and consequence of the arms race. "It is part of the general pattern of misguided policy," claimed General Douglas MacArthur, "that our country is geared to an arms economy which was bred in an artificially induced psychosis of war hysteria and nurtured upon an incessant propaganda of fear."
See BALANCE OF TERROR.

FEDERAL EMERGENCY MANAGEMENT AGENCY (FEMA). The shades of Pollyanna; an institutional paragon of rose-colored asses who try to make nuclear war look both livable and lovable. A 1982 FEMA White House "Food Vulnerability Briefing," for example, considered the effects of a 1,200-warhead, 6,000-megaton attack on the U.S. agricultural system. The good news was that, although 46 percent of the U.S. population would perish, survival rates would be better for livestock and the rural population. Fortunately, too, "the number of survivors during the first sixty days following an attack drops over time. Thus, those who are doomed to die will be consumers for [only] part of that time." Unfortunately, however, nuclear war could disrupt food processing and distribution. FEMA notes that "the margin of safety in the ratio of potentially surviving processing capabilities to surviving population is razor thin." Too, the success of FEMA's post-attack farm scenario depends on the failure of crisis relocation. "Ironically," the report notes, "the relatively favorable balance between population and livestock and poultry survival rates expected under current Civil Defense capabilities could disappear under an effective crisis relocation plan."
See CIVIL DEFENSE, CRISIS RELOCATION, NUCLEAR WINTER, POST-ATTACK RECOVERY SCENARIO, SCENARIO.

FIREBALL. The helliosphere of a nuclear explosion, whose fire and brimstone create an earthly inferno. The fireball of a 25 megaton bomb reaches temperatures of 200,000,000 degrees Fahrenheit, vaporizes everything within 6 miles, incinerates everything within a 30-mile radius, and burns people within 80 miles. Anyone glancing at the fireball, a normal human reaction, would suffer retinal burns and blindness--as far away as 40 miles.
See FIRESTORM, FLASHBLINDNESS, HELL.

FIREBREAK. The space between the rungs of the escalation ladder that theoretically makes it possible to use it as a fire escape. The most important firebreak is between conventional and nuclear war; NATO's first use policy makes it a firetrap.
See ESCALATION LADDER, FIRST USE, NUCLEAR THRESHOLD.

FIRESTORM. An infernal combustion engine that drives a holocaust, in the root sense of the word, "burnt whole." The fireball of an urban nuclear explosion sets off gas stations, natural gas lines, oil storage tanks, automobile gas tanks, and other flash points, as well as less flammable materials like wood, cloth, and paper. As these fires burn, the hot air rises, cooler air is whipped into the fire zone, and hurricane-force winds bring more oxygen to fan the flames. Temperatures rise to 1,600 degrees Fahrenheit, and even people in shelters are baked or asphyxiated. The Hiroshima firestorm destroyed 2,800 acres, but a 20-megaton bomb could ravage an area 500 times larger.
See FIREBALL, NUCLEAR EXPLOSION.

FIRST STRIKE. The first pitch of the last inning of the World Serious, specifically a surprise attack on an opponent's nuclear arsenal designed to eliminate the possibility of reprisal.
See COUNTERFORCE, DECAPITATION, PRE-EMPTIVE STRIKE.

FIRST USE. The first firing of nuclear weapons, strategic or tactical, under any circumstances. In 1981, Soviet Premier Breshnev committed the USSR to a "no-first-use" policy, but the US and NATO rely on the first use of tactical weapons to stop a Soviet onslaught in Europe. Abbreviated "fuse," because this first fire could very well detonate the planet.
See FIRST STRIKE, NO FIRST USE.

FISSION. A process of bombarding atomic nuclei in order to produce enough energy to bombard people. Neutrons split the nucleus of heavy atoms of uranium or plutonium, releasing more neutrons and the immense force that normally binds atoms together. At Armageddon, God will probably post a sign on the earth, saying simply, "Gone fission."
See ATOM, CHAIN REACTION, FUSION, REACTOR.

FLASHBLINDNESS. The temporary sightlessness that succeeds a look at a nuclear explosion, as opposed to the congenital myopia that precedes it.

FLEXIBLE RESPONSE. NATO's elastic claws, fitted over the mailed fist of massive retaliation; a military policy promising reprisal--conventional and/or nuclear--for any Soviet aggression, up to and including the irresponse of Armageddon.
See COUNTERVAILING STRATEGY, ESCALATION, ESCALATION LADDER, MASSIVE RETALIATION, NATO.

FLEXIBLE TARGETING. Targeting inclusive enough to provide missions for the surplus warheads manufactured in the 1970s; the counterpoise of counterforce and countervalue strategies in American strategic doctrine; thus, since 1974, U.S. missiles have targeted both Soviet cities _and_ military installations.
--syn. Nu-Opts.
See COUNTERFORCE, COUNTERVAILING STRATEGY, COUNTERVALUE, NU-OPTS.

FORCE STRUCTURE. The size and shape of the military might that might adjust the size and shape of everything else. American nuclear force structure, for example, is built on the triad, while Soviet nuclear force structure emphasizes ICBMs and SLBMs more than bomber forces.
See TRIAD, WEAPONS MIX.

FORWARD BASED SYSTEMS. American sub-strategic weapons systems that can strike Soviet territory, because they are based in contiguous countries or on aircraft carriers. These systems--like F-111s in England, and F-4 Phantom fighter bombers and A-6 and A-7 attack bombers on aircraft carriers in the North Atlantic and Mediterranean--have been the foreword to froward negotiations, because the USSR has no comparable capability.
See MEDIUM BOMBER.

FRACTIONATION. A process of multiplication by division, multiplying murders by dividing the payload of a missile into several warheads.
See MIRV.

FRANCK REPORT. A frank 1945 report from a scientific committee on Social and Political Implications of the Bomb to Secretary of War Henry Stimson. The report declared that "the use of nuclear bombs for an early unannounced attack against Japan is inadvisable. If the U.S. were to be the first to release this new means of indiscriminate destruction upon mankind, she would sacrifice public support throughout the world, precipitate the race for armaments, and prejudice the possibility of reaching an international agreement on the future control of such weapons."

FRATRICIDE. 1. The act of killing one's brother; 2. The unintentional destruction of one bomb by the effects--blast, radiation, and debris--of another bomb at the same target; 3. The foundation for dense pack MX missile basing, in which American missiles would be placed so close together that Soviet warheads would commit fratricide before hitting the American missiles. Fratricide, therefore, makes the world safe for genocide.
See DENSE PACK, MX.

Tony Auth. The Philadelphia Inquirer. Reprinted with permission.

FREE WORLD. The world of free enterprise, in which the market mechanism allocates injustice; as opposed to socialism, in which the state does.
See IRON CURTAIN, PROFIT.

FUSION. 1. The source of the sun's energy; 2. The sun-day special at the atomic cafe, a combination platter created when the chef puts deuterium or tritium in an oven heated by an atomic explosion. The separate nuclei melt together, losing mass, and freeing immense amounts of energy.
See FISSION, HYDROGEN BOMB.

GAME THEORY. A way of playing the policy game by the numbers; the mathematical analysis of strategy to determine the best game plan for a country to be number one without its number coming up.
See EXPERT, WAR GAMES.

GENERAL AND COMPLETE DISARMAMENT. An obsolete appellation for the "unrealistic" sort of disarmament that would make generals obsolete; the elimination of weapons and military forces (except police) by all nations at the same time; the overall (though overlooked) goal of Soviet-American arms control, according to the McCloy-Zorin Principles of 1961.
See ARMS CONTROL, DISARMAMENT, IDEALISM, REALISM.

GENOCIDE. The systematic killing or extermination of a people or a nation, usually used in reference to the Nazi slaughter of 6 million Jews. The US Office of Technology Assessment estimates that nuclear attack on a range of military and economic targets using a large fraction of existing arsenals would kill 20 to 160 million people, regardless of race, color, or creed.
See COLLATERAL DAMAGE, MAD, UNACCEPTABLE DAMAGE.

GODLESS. 1. An immoderate modifier of "communism," which allows godly Americans to ignore God's commandments--most notably "Love thy neighbor as thyself"--in dealing with the Soviets; 2. The adjectival assumption that, because some Communists do not love God, God does not love them.
See ENEMY, SIN, SOVIET THREAT.

GRADUATED DETERRENCE. The active ingradient of flexible response; the ability to commence nuclear war by degrees.
See DETERRENCE, ESCALATION LADDER, FLEXIBLE RESPONSE, INTRAWAR DETERRENCE.

GROUND ALERT. The condition of bomber readiness that assures that 30 percent of U.S. B-52s will be in the air when their bases become ground zero.
--syn. strip alert.
See GROUND ZERO.

GROUND ZERO. The precise site of a nuclear explosion, at which the whole is reduced to the sum of its parts, which is zero. Human beings at ground zero literally vaporize, as temperatures of 10,000,000 degrees Fahrenheit broil the body (which is mostly water) from solidity to steam.
--syn. hypocenter.
See FIREBALL.

GUERNICA. A peace of art by Pablo Picasso depicting the horrors of area bombing.
See AREA BOMBING.

HALF-LIFE. 1. The time it takes a radioisotope to decrease to half its original radioactivity, e.g., for plutonium, 24000 years; 2. The state or condition of people threatened by radioactive wastes, either in the form of nuclear weapons or fission byproducts.
See WASTE.

HARD TARGET. The postwar equivalent of the Maginot Line, a set of blockhouses designed by blockheads; concrete silos and command posts reinforced with steel to withstand pressures of 2000 pounds per square inch.
--syn. point target.
See SILO, SOFT TARGET.

HARD TARGET CAPABILITY. The ability to supersoften superhardened targets with weapons of high lethality in a counterforce strike.
--syn. first strike capability.
See COUNTERFORCE, FIRST STRIKE, HARD TARGET, HARDENED, LETHALITY, TIME- URGENT HARD TARGET KILL CAPABILITY.

HARDENED. 1. The state or condition of missile silos, command posts, or buildings that have been reinforced with steel and concrete to withstand the blast of a nuclear bomb; 2. The state or condition of people who have been forced to consider how their bodies will withstand the blast of a nuclear bomb.
See HARD TARGET, SOFT TARGET.

HEAVY BOMBER. The weighty term for the round trip service of Intercontinental Airlines; a bomber like the B-52 that can waste the enemy's homeland and return to the wasteland of home.
--syn. strategic bomber.
See B-1, MEDIUM BOMBER.

HELL. The earth, during and after nuclear war.

HIGH FRONTIER. 1. The highflown euphuism for a strategic highflyer; 2. That area above the atmosphere where the spacey minds of think tanks hope to fight a nuclear war; 3. The proposed American strategic defense initiative, consisting of a space-based ballistic missile defense, a broader space protection system of beam weapons, a ground-based point defense, and an active program of civil defense.

Daniel O. Graham, the Director of Project High Frontier at the Heritage Foundation, claims that "we can escape the brooding menace of 'balance of terror' doctrines by deploying defensive systems in space. We can confound the prophets of doom by opening the vast and rich High Frontier of space for industrialization."
See ABM, BALANCE OF TERROR, BMD, DAMAGE LIMITATION, STAR WARS, THINK TANK.

HIROSHIMA. 1. The first boom town of the nuclear age, in which 100,000 people reaped the dividends of the enrichment of uranium. 2. "We need Hiroshima to give substance to our terror," says Robert Jay Lifton, "however inadequately that city can represent what would happen now if thermonuclear weapons were to be used on human populations."
See NAGASAKI.

HOLOCAUST. The wholesale cost of the product of the costive minds of the Pentagon, i.e. nuclear war.
See GENOCIDE, NUCLEAR WINTER.

HORIZONTAL ESCALATION. According to Jonathan Green, "a situation in which the response to one crisis is to initiate another one elsewhere."
See ESCALATION, ESCALATION DOMINANCE, ESCALATION LADDER.

HOSTAGES. People interned by threat of interment as "security" for extortion; specifically the potential victims of the countervalue strike that ensues from deterrence and mutually assured destruction. In the atomic age, we are all hostages to this misfortune.
--syn. human beings.
See CITIZENS.

HOT. A new usage for an old adjective, by which the the lethal radioactivity of some materials is compared to the warmth of others. Lacking the prestige of jargon, this use of familiar words for unfamiliar phenomena is still a form of nukespeak, because the language fails to convey the singularity of the situation.
See RADIATION.

HOTLINE. A direct teletype connection between Moscow and Washington to assure that neither will reach out and torch someone. The U.S. hotline occupies a "soft" command post in the Pentagon, where it will be destroyed. Thus, should a nuclear war begin, communications will stop cold (except for C3I), and the hotline will simply be "hot."
See CONFIDENCE BUILDING MEASURES, WAR TERMINATION.

HUMAN RIGHTS. Those natural rights to life, liberty, and the pursuit of happiness in a free enterprise system that are the cause and casualty of national rites of war.
See FREE WORLD.

HUNGER. The state or condition of emptiness of the stomach and/or the spirit caused by the glut of nuclear weapons in the body politic.
See REAGAN(AT)OMICS.

HYDROGEN BOMB. The fusion-powered combine that improves the efficiency of the Grim Reaper by converting the matter of hydrogen isotopes into energy.
--syn. thermonuclear bomb.
See FISSION, FUSION.

IDEALISM. The belief that what should be could be.
See REALISM.

INNOCENT BYSTANDER. An oxymoron that occludes the minds of morons who think that megadeath is not part of the American way of life. Ignoring the nuclear evil, they are ignorant but not innocent; bystanding still, they push the arms race toward the point where ignorance is blast.
See MEGADEATH, SIN.

Hunger

--from <u>Herblock</u> <u>on</u> <u>All</u> <u>Fronts</u> (New American Library, 1980)

INTEGRATED BATTLEFIELD. A battlefield on which conventional, nuclear, and bio-chemical weapons are combined to enhance the separate but equal slaughter of soldiers. The troops then reside in an intergrated neighborhood.
See RACISM.

INTERIM STORAGE. The cache cropper of nuclear waste, a method of stashing radioactive trash for the indefinite interval until a procedure for permanent disposal is devised and employed.
See NUCLEAR FUEL CYCLE, PERMANENT DISPOSAL, WASTE.

INTERSERVICE RIVALRY. The hot war of the Cold War, a battle fought by the Army, Navy, and Air Force to see who will get more bucks for the bang.
See DEPARTMENT OF DEFENSE, PENTAGON.

INTRAWAR DETERRENCE. A method of post-partum death control; the process of preventing the escalation of a war which the same process has failed to prevent.
--syn. escalation control.
See DETERRENCE.

IRON CURTAIN. 1. The metaphorical boundary between the Communist Bloc (in irons) and the Free World (with its irons in the fire), maintained by a containment policy on both sides; 2. The blinds used in the ironic game of blindman's buffer, in which blindfolded players race to catch each other off balance.
See BALANCE OF TERROR, CONTAINMENT, FREE WORLD.

JOKE. A laughingstock who would say--even in jest-- "My fellow Americans, I am pleased to tell you I have just signed legislation which outlaws Russia forever. The bombing begins in five minutes." Despite its funhouse character, such a joke makes the audience wonder if the joker is wild. See REAGANSPEAK.

Oliphant by Pat Oliphant. (c) 1984. Universal Press Syndicate. All rights reserved. Reprinted with permission.

JUST WAR. An international joust justified by chivalrous adherence to codes of battle established in the Middle Ages.
--ant. nuclear war.
See BISHOPS.

JUSTICE. The sine qua non of peace, the World's Fare when the world's fair. "I tremble for my country," said Thomas Jefferson, "when I think that God is just."
See PEACE.

KILLING. An obsolete word, "neutralized" in State Department human rights reports as "unlawful or arbitrary deprivation of life."
See EUPHEMISM, HUMAN RIGHTS.

KILOTON. An abbreviated version of kill-o-ton; the explosive equivalent of 1,000 tons of TNT.
See MEGATON.

KNEECAP. A prosthetic device for the Achilles' heel of the White House; the National Emergency Command Post, a Boeing 747 fitted with a Presidential suite, a red phone, and a wall of display screens, for fighting a nuclear war after the washout of Washington.
See LOOKING GLASS.

LAUNCH CONTROL CENTER. A command center designed to "control" Minuteman missiles by launching them.
See LAUNCH CONTROL OFFICER.

LAUNCH CONTROL OFFICER. The key link in the chain of command from the President to the apocalypse, the man who turns the key that opens the pandours' box of nuclear missiles.
See BLACK BRIEFCASE, LAUNCH CONTROL CENTER.

LAUNCH ON WARNING. The hair trigger on the gun in the game of Russian-American roulette, a procedure whereby computers fire missiles as soon as radar detects an incoming attack of missiles, the moon, or aggressive geese. As counterforce weapons proliferate, launch on warning looks more likely.
--syn. doomsday device.
--ant. crisis stability, fail-safe, ride out.
See ACCIDENTAL WAR, COMPUTER ERROR, DOOMSDAY DEVICE, FAIL-SAFE.

LEAKAGE. 1. A linguistic seeping pill, which, when plumbed, means a missile or missiles that penetrates all lines of defense to hit its target. Given the holes in ABM and air defense, we could all drown in this leakage; 2. The release of politically sensitive information to citizens; the Defense Department, for one, plans to plug these leaks by widespread use of polygraph tests.

LETHALITY. A mathematical measure of the ability of a missile, through combined accuracy and yield, to destroy hard targets. Curiously, although it derives from an adjective ("lethal") applied to things that purposefully cause death, "lethality" does not refer to the ability of a missile aimed at a hard target to kill people. That is called "collateral damage."
See CEP, COLLATERAL DAMAGE, SURVIVABILITY.

LEUKEMIA. The abiding blood bath of the Cold War; a cancer caused by radiation exposure that cripples blood-forming tissues and immune systems.
See RADIATION SICKNESS.

LIMITED NUCLEAR WAR. A comfortably qualified expression for any atomic engagement with survivors; thus a war limited only by the inhibition or inability to annihilate all life. Two popular scenarios for limited nuclear war are, first, a war that devastates only the continent of Europe, and second, a war in which the superpowers mutually restrain themselves to selective strikes. In the first instance, the war will not seem limited to those within its limits. In the second instance, as many as 20 million people are expected to die in both countries.
See NUCLEAR WARFIGHTING.

Reprinted with permission of the Minneapolis Star and Tribune.

LIMITED TEST BAN. A 1963 agreement between the US and the USSR to prohibit nuclear tests in the atmosphere, above the atmosphere, or in the seas in order to prevent the proliferation of nuclear weapons. The treaty was "limited," not so much because it limited testing, but because it did not limit testing underground. In fact, in order to secure the support of the Joint Chiefs of Staff, President John Kennedy had to promise to continue testing, and both the US and the USSR accelerated their test programs after 1963.
See ARMS CONTROL, COMPREHENSIVE TEST BAN, TESTING.

LINKAGE. The connection between nuclear issues and other international behavior of the Soviet Union; the idea that permits us to avoid all negotiation with the USSR until the situation is so good that negotiations are unnecessary.
See ARMS CONTROL.

LITTLE BOY. 1. A small male child; 2. The small bomb (12 pounds of uranium 235 in an 8,000 pound projectile) that killed thousands of little boys and girls and their parents at Hiroshima.
See BOY, HIROSHIMA.

LOCA. A loss-of-coolant accident in which the core of a nuclear reactor is exposed to air and a corps of human beings is exposed to death. If a LOCA cannot be contained, a meltdown results.
See MELTDOWN, NORMAL ABERRATION, THREE MILE ISLAND.

LOOKING GLASS. The Alice-in-Wonderland nickname for the airborne command post (now renamed Cover All) that allows SAC to conduct a nuclear war after its headquarters has been destroyed. The pilot of

this plane has perfect vision, but he wears an eyepatch over one eye so that, if he is blinded by the flash of a nuclear explosion, he can switch to the other eye and continue to blindly follow orders to extract an eye for an eye and a tooth for a tooth from the enemy.
--syn. doomsday plane.
See C3I, STRATEGIC AIR COMMAND.

MAD. 1. Mutually Assured Destruction, the death insurance policy that keeps deterrence alive; 2. Mentally ill, crazy, insane; 3. A magazine whose mascot expresses our atomic insanity with the question "What--me worry?" 4. The wrath of people who pay the premiums for the policy of MAD--with their money and their lives.
See SANE.

MAJOR ATTACK OPTION. The "football" option play in which the Yankee quarterback throws more than a thousand bombs at the opposing side in order to reach the end zone.
See BLACK BRIEFCASE, NU-OPTS.

MANHATTAN PROJECT. The nom de guerre of the World War II American bomb-building program, which has resulted in a Promethean program to raze cities, both by siphoning resources from urban social services, and by blasting away the need for any social services.
See HIROSHIMA, NAGASAKI.

MARV. Maneuverable Re-entry Vehicle; the marvelous MIRV that can be electronically guided precisely to its targets.
See TERCOM.

MASSIVE RETALIATION. An I for an eye, and a town for a tooth; a policy of wholesale massacre for retail transgressions.
See COUNTERVALUE, DETERRENCE, MAD, MINIMUM DETERRENCE.

MEASURED RESPONSE. A modern military doctrine that dictates a response to military attack by limited military means in an effort to avoid escalation to total war. The doctrine was not in effect in 1960, when SAC commander Tommy Powers asked, "Why do you want to restrain ourselves? Restraint! Why are you so concerned with saving their lives? The whole idea is to kill the bastards."
--syn. controlled response.
See COUNTERFORCE, NU-OPTS.

MEDICINE. The science and art of saving lives, which--like the rest of us--will take its medicine in a nuclear war. In Hiroshima, 270 of 298 doctors and 1,645 of 1,780 nurses died in the blast; 42 of 45 hospitals were destroyed. Doctors who would be dead realize that "we as physicians can do virtually nothing in the case of explosion of nuclear weapons," and have formed Physicians for Social Responsibility to practice preventive medicine.

MEDIUM BOMBER. Bombers that have intercontinental round-trip range with refueling, but not without.
See BACKFIRE, HEAVY BOMBER.

MEGADEATH. A singular noun for one million corpses.
See GENOCIDE.

MEGATON. The explosive force of a million tons of TNT, which, when wielded by megalomaniacs, could doom us all to a megalosaurian fate. One megaton of TNT would fill a freight train 250 miles long; a freight train filled with 15 megatons of TNT could have its engine in New York and its caboose in San Francisco. A 1-megaton explosion is like 70 simultaneous Hiroshima bombs; a 20-megaton bomb represents 1,400 Hiroshima bombs at the same time and place. But American and Soviet arsenals contain more than 13 thousand megatons of nuclear weapons.
See KILOTON, MEGADEATH.

MELTDOWN. 1. The liquefaction of the core of a nuclear reactor due to loss of coolant; 2. The ensuing liquidation of public trust in nuclear safety.
See CHINA SYNDROME, LOCA, THREE MILE ISLAND.

MICROCEPHALY. A birth defect caused by irradiation of fetuses by nuclear weapons employed by the acrocephalic experts of the think tanks and the Pentagon. Irradiated babies also suffer disproportionately from myopia, liver cirrhosis, tuberculosis, and other malformations.
See EXPERT, MUTATION, RADIATION SICKNESS, THINK TANK.

MIDGETMAN. A single-headed dwarf missile whose mobility reduces its vulnerability and its verifiability. Midgetman would close both the window of vulnerability and the window of opportunity for arms control.
See MX, SCOWCROFT COMMISSION, VERIFICATION, VULNERABILITY, WINDOW OF VULNERABILITY.

"WHY COULDN'T YOU HAVE JUST SAID YOU LEF YOUR APPLE ON THE HOT PLATE INSTEAD OF 'THERE'S BEEN A CORE MELTDOWN'?"

MILITARY-INDUSTRIAL COMPLEX. 1. The marital contract between business and the brass, by which they mutually pledge to propagate generations of new weapons that threaten both reproduction and future generations; 2. The headlock of this wedlock; a widespread psychological syndrome characterized by the belief that the bottom line of this "business as usual" is not the ground zero of a grave.

According to Leon Wieseltier, "The USA and the USSR do not <u>have</u> military-industrial complexes: they <u>are</u> such complexes." Among the corporations that manufacture the hydrogen bomb are, for example, General Electric ("Progress for People"), Monsanto ("Without chemicals, life itself would be impossible"), DuPont ("The leading edge"), Rockwell International ("Where science gets down to business"), Union Carbide ("Today, something we do will touch your life"), Bendix ("We speak technology"), Western Electric, a subsidiary of AT&T ("The system is the solution"), and the University of California ("Let there be light").
See BUY-IN, PROFIT.

MINIMUM DETERRENCE. The strategy, based on the maxim that a punch of prevention is worth a pounding of cure, that deters attack by maximizing death and destruction, minimizing only the number of missiles needed to do it. A strategy of minimum deterrence would permit massive disarmament, because one Poseidon submarine, for example, carries enough warheads to destroy every large and medium-sized city in the USSR.
--syn. finite deterrence
See COUNTERVALUE, DETERRENCE, MAD, MASSIVE RETALIATION, UNILATERAL DISARMAMENT.

MINI-NUKE. A baby nuclear weapon, the delivery of which is not birth, but death.
See TACTICAL NUCLEAR WEAPONS.

MINUTEMAN. 1. A person prepared at a minute's notice to risk life by fighting an 18th-century super-power for the cause of freedom; 2. A missile prepared by a 20th-century superpower to take life at a minute's notice for the cause of freedom, national interest, or credibility.
See CREDIBILITY, MIDGETMAN, NATIONAL INTEREST.

MIRV. Nickname for Multiple Independently Targetable Reentry Vehicle, a hydra-(war)headed missile that allows the arms race to accelerate in an era of arms control. When the SALT treaties delimited delivery vehicles, the US and the USSR re-entered the race with re-entry vehicles. The result was increased lethality, counterforce capability, and instability. Henry Kissinger, who approved the US move to MIRVs, said later, "I wish I had thought through the implications of a MIRVed world," namely offensive capabilities and incentives to make men and missiles defenseless.
See MX.

MISSILE GAP. The gap between the ears of those who think that the window of vulnerability is a new idea. In 1960, John F. Kennedy ran for the presidency accusing the Republicans of allowing a "missile gap" with the Soviet Union. Subsequent analysis showed that there had been no gap—indeed, the United States had 6500 deliverable warheads to the Soviet Union's 300—but Kennedy closed it anyway, embarking on an unprecedented buildup of Minuteman ICBMs and Polaris SLBMs.
See BOMBER GAP, WINDOW OF VULNERABILITY.

MODERNIZATION. The process of improving nuclear weapons so that, as Winston Churchill said, "the Stone Age may return on the gleaming wings of science."
See BUILD-DOWN, TESTING.

MONEY. The medium of exchange we burn in buying the weapons whose exchange will burn us.
See NUCLEAR EXCHANGE, PROFITS, TAXES, TRUST.

MUF. Material Unaccounted For, a muff of the nuclear safeguards system that could result in diversion of special nuclear material to irresponsible terrorists, and in the divulsion of irresolvable innocents.
--syn. book-physical inventory difference.
See NUCLEAR SAFEGUARDS.

MUNICH. A Bavarian city that will be obliterated by nuclear weapons unless the Western powers learn to lessen the lesson of Munich: that negotiation with the enemy is synonymous with appeasement. Otherwise, the slogan "No more Munichs" will, sooner or later, mean no more Munich.
See APPEASEMENT.

MURDER. According to Webster, murder is the unlawful killing of another human being with malice aforethought. The key word here is "unlawful;" if the laws support plans for homicide--even genocide--then you <u>can</u> "get away with murder."
See SIN, TAXES.

MURPHY'S LAW. If something can go wrong, it will.
See ACCIDENTAL WAR, COMPUTER ERROR, FAIL-SAFE, NORMAL ABERRATION, THREE MILE ISLAND.

MUSHROOM CLOUD. A giant <u>tod</u>-stool that grows on the site or a nuclear explosion, sucking death and debris into a radioactive cloud that drops death and debris downwind from ground zero.
See FALLOUT, GROUND ZERO, RADIATION SICKNESS.

MUTATION. The genetic process by which radiation transforms the offspring of mutes into mutants.
See APATHY, CITIZENS, INNOCENT BYSTANDER, RADIATION SICKNESS.

HE'S GROWN A FOOT SINCE I SAW HIM LAST....

MX. 1. Missile experimental; an elaborate experiment to see if Congress and the American people will buy a weapon that both enables and invites a first strike; 2. A deci-MIRVed missile that can literally deci-mate 10 hard or soft targets. Designed to match the Soviet SS-18 and to close the window of vulnerability, the MX missile has counterforce capability (like the SS-18) which, with its 10 warheads, makes it an inviting target for attack, especially in the Minuteman silos that supposedly made our missile force vulnerable in the first place. Although the missile is a destabilizing weapon, President Reagan has promoted this "Peacekeeper" as a bargaining chip in arms control negotiations. Said he, "A vote against MX production today is a vote against arms control tomorrow."

See ARMS CONTROL, BARGAINING CHIPS, DENSE PACK, DESTABILIZING WEAPONS, EXCHANGE RATIO, FIRST STRIKE, MIRV, PEACEKEEPER, REAGANSPEAK, SCOWCROFT COMMISSION, WINDOW OF VULNERABILITY.

Reprinted with permission of the Minneapolis Star and Tribune.

NAGASAKI. An urban hibachi, in which more than a million pounds of human flesh were grilled on August 9, 1945.
See HIROSHIMA.

NATIONAL INTEREST. 1. An interest at odds with the international interest, which is that national interests do not explode into war; 2. The money paid to service the national debt, which is increased by defense spending to protect the national interest.

NATIONAL SECURITY. The red, white, and blue blanket that Americans wear over their heads to hide the atomic arrows clutched in the claws of the American eagle. The national security blanket blinds people to their preparations for genocide, and suffocates critical questioning. Fortunately, it may also serve as a shroud for Americans massacred in the name of their national security. Then, and only then, they will be secure in the root meaning of the word--"free of care."
--ant. personal security.

NATIONAL TECHNICAL MEANS. "A euphemism for finding out what the Russians are doing without any help from the Russians," says Robert Kaiser; a <u>technical</u> term that <u>means</u> satellites, radars, and radio receivers that can verify arms control agreements. See VERIFICATION.

NATIONAL WILL. 1. The will to deceive; specifically the determination to convince the enemy that we will stop at nothing--even stupidity or suicide-- to prevent them from murdering us; 2. An expression of futurity endangered by the fatuity of those people determined to demonstrate their will; 3. The legal document detailing the disposition of the pulverized property of the corpse of the body politic after its demise in a nuclear war; 4. George Will.
See CREDIBILITY.

NATO. North Atlantic Treaty Organization, a combination of American and West European nations formed in 1949 to deter Communist expansion by threatening the commination of the Commie nations.
--ant. Warsaw Pact.
See CONTAINMENT.

NEUTRON BOMB. According to the Pentagon, "an efficient nuclear weapon that eliminates an enemy with a minimum amount of damage to friendly territory;" a nuclear weapon designed primarily to stop a tank attack in Western Europe by bombarding Soviet soldiers with deadly neutron radiation.
See CLEAN BOMB, ENHANCED RADIATION WEAPON.

Paul Szep. The Boston Globe. Reprinted with permission.

NEWSPEAK. 1. In Orwell's <u>1984</u>, a language "designed not to extend but to <u>diminish</u> the range of thought"; 2. The language of TV news, which informs its audience by dividing its attention among 15 to 20 "stories" of what's "new," each averaging 30 to 60 seconds, and presented with impassive "objectivity." In 1982, for example, network news reports from the USSR totaled just 60 minutes for the year. And the American public responds predictably: they watch the news "show," patronize its sponsors, and--within 30 minutes--forget what they have seen.
See CITIZENS, DOUBLESPEAK.

NO FIRST USE. A dress rehearsal of "Promises, Promises"; a pledge of allegiance to the flag of conventional warfare, at least until the rockets' red glare shows the enemy on the far side of the nuclear firebreak. The USSR has taken the pledge; the United States--because of its dependence on tactical nuclear weapons in Europe--has not.
See FIREBREAK, FIRST USE.

NON-PROLIFERATION TREATY. A contraceptive device to prevent the propagation of weapons and the population explosion of nuclear war by encouraging the continence of countries.
See PROLIFERATION.

NORMAL ABERRATION. A phrase coined by the nuclear industry after Three Mile Island to denote a nuclear accident. While it is intended to be euphemistic and reassuring, the normalcy of aberration is abhorrent.
--syn. abnormal evolution, event, plant transient.
See ENERGETIC DISASSEMBLY, MELTDOWN, THREE MILE ISLAND.

NUCLEAR CLUB. 1. The "big stick" of atomic diplomacy, i.e., the atomic bomb; 2. The group of nations or persons in possession of the nuclear club. Members presently include (in order of successful application) the United States, the USSR, Great Britain, France, China, and India, but many others are clamoring for admittance, including Israel and South Africa, both of which may have surreptitiously joined.
See PROLIFERATION.

NUCLEAR EXCHANGE. The change that will make an "ex" of all of us; the reciprocal gift of death and destruction from detonated nuclear weapons, wrapped in a tissue of lies, packaged in scenarios, and tied with a euphemistic bow.
--ant. cultural exchange.
See DELIVERY SYSTEM, SCENARIO.

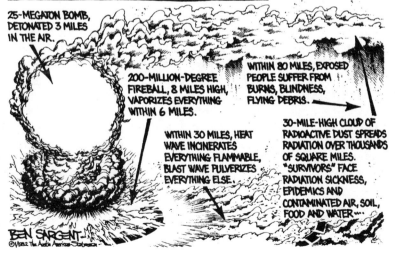

Reprinted with permission from the Austin American Statesman.

NUCLEAR EXPLOSION. A dishonorable discharge from deterrence, described--for a single 1-megaton bomb on one city--by David Barash and Judith Lipton:

"The bomb explodes with the heat of the sun and the stars, and within the first 2 seconds, the center of the city, including steel and concrete buildings, asphalt, roads, bridges, brick, glass, people, plants, and animals are vaporized. If a groundburst, the center of the city is turned into a crater, 1000 feet in diameter and 200 feet deep, surrounded by a rim of highly radioactive debris of about twice this diameter.

"Within the first 2 seconds after the detonation, the fireball grows rapidly, emitting gamma rays and neutrons, as well as infrared radiation, pulsing outward at the speed of light. The blinding flash melts the eyeballs of anyone looking on from close to the explosion, and causes retinal burns to anyone who reflexively glances at it from within 50 miles. Within a radius of 1.75 miles, steel surfaces evaporate, concrete surfaces explodes, glass melts, and people are melted and then charred. At 2.75 miles, aluminum siding evaporates, auto sheet metal and lucite windows melt. (People fare no better.) At 4.35 miles, wood, plastics, and heavy fabrics burst into flames, and asphalt surfaces melt. At 5.5 miles from the detonation, upholstery, canvas, and clothing burst into flames, and painted surfaces explode. Watching the destruction of a city with a nuclear bomb, one would see it melt, char, then collapse. An individual human being, say two miles from ground zero, within the first two seconds would receive fatal total body irradiation, plus third degree burns. Her clothing would

catch fire, along with her skin, and she would quickly be reduced to a charred corpse."
See AIR BURST, BLAST WAVE, FALLOUT, FIREBALL, FIRESTORM, GROUND BURST, MEGADEATH.

NUCLEAR FAMILY. Mom, Dad, and the kids; the main target of nuclear bombs.
See BOY, LITTLE BOY, PARENTS.

THe NuCLeAR FAMILY

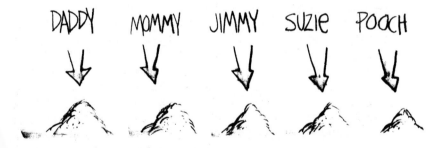

Pat Bagley. Reprinted with permission of Peregrine Smith Books.

NUCLEAR FREE ZONE. An area freed from the production and deployment of nuclear weapons, but not from the consequences of their use, which will be worldwide.
See NUCLEAR WINTER.

NUCLEAR FREEZE. Making the Cold War colder by icing
the arms race; a pre-emptive strike on weapons
modernization; specifically a proposal for a bilateral, mutually verifiable halt of the testing,
production, and deployment of nuclear weapons at
current levels of approximate parity, before nego-
tiating to reduce weapon stockpiles.
--ant. nuclear winter.
See COMPREHENSIVE TEST BAN.

Ed Stein. Rocky Mountain News. Reprinted with permission.

NUCLEAR FRIEZE. The handwriting on the wall;
silhouettes of vaporized people and objects that
are etched in concrete by an atomic fireball.
See FIREBALL.

NUCLEAR FUEL CYCLE. An unsteady vehicle for transforming innocuous elements such as uranium into deadly radioactive wastes. Peddled by the nuclear industry, with the human race as passengers, this no-wealed vehicle also emits heat which is used to boil water or broil people.
See ENRICHED URANIUM, REACTOR, WASTE.

NUCLEAR PACIFISTS. Peace-loving people who want to make the world safe for conventional weapons.
See CONVENTIONAL WEAPONS, PACIFISTS.

NUCLEAR SAFEGUARDS. Procedures designed to assuage public anxiety by deterring and/or detecting diversion of "special nuclear material" to potential bomb-builders. "'Safeguard' is a misnomer, connoting more 'safety' and 'guarding' than is warranted," said Senator John Glenn in 1981. "The system basically consists of information gathering and reporting--nothing more."
--syn. public diplomacy
See CREDIBILITY, FAIL-SAFE, MUF.

NUCLEAR THRESHOLD. The claptrap door to nuclear war, the doorway to doomsday; the point at which a conventional war "goes nuclear" and a conventional world goes "boom."
See FIREBREAK.

NUCLEAR UMBRELLA. The postwar model of British Prime Minister Neville Chamberlain's parasol, the nuclear umbrella is a bombershoot aimed at the Soviet Union to shield Europe from a precipitous nuclear rain from the East.
See APPEASEMENT, MUNICH, NATO.

NUCLEAR WAR. An idea whose time is, unfortunately, coming. According to Sydney J. Harris, the idea of nuclear war is a Rorschach test for Americans:
"'Nuclear war is inevitable,' says the pessimist.
'Nuclear war is impossible,' says the optimist.
'Nuclear war is inevitable unless we make it impossible,' says the realist."
See OPTIMIST, PESSIMIST, REALISM.

NUCLEAR WARFIGHTING. The fight plan for the day after deterrence; a strategy for prolonged nuclear conflict that features counterforce targeting for prevailing in a nuclear war. In 1982, SAC Commander Bennie Davis told Congress that the U.S. had dropped MAD "at least two years ago" for a policy of "counterforce" and "warfighting." "The two," he said, "are synonymous."
--syn. flexible nuclear response, limited nuclear options, nu-opts, Schlesinger Doctrine.
See COUNTERFORCE, FLEXIBLE TARGETING, MAD, NU-OPTS, WIN.

NUCLEAR WINTER. The winter of our discontent, when the mushroom clouds of dust and debris blanket the earth, blocking the rays of the sun, lowering temperatures, destroying agriculture, and starving the human survivors. The phenomenon of nuclear winter gives new meaning, therefore, to the slogan "Freeze now or freeze later!"
See ECOCIDE, NUCLEAR FREEZE.

NUKE. As a noun, a nuclear weapon; as a verb, to destroy with nuclear weapons; the four-letter word of nuclear newspeak. The ultimate transitive verb, it takes all objects. A noun for the nonce, since it foreshortens the future.

NU-OPTS. The optical illusion that added options for beginning a nuclear exchange optimize the chances for ending it. President Nixon and Defense Secretary James Schlesinger opted for Nu-Opts in 1974, because it provides, in the jargon, "a richer menu of attack options" to cannibalize the enemy.
--syn. flexible nuclear response, limited nuclear options, Schlesinger Doctrine.
See COUNTERFORCE, COUNTERVAILING STRATEGY.

OPTIMIST. A person who believes that this is the best of all possible worlds.
See IDEALISM, PESSIMIST, REALISM.

OVERKILL. 1. The "once is not enough" of nuclear necrophilia; a type of serial murder in which the victim is killed again and again and again; 2. The ability to inflict such hypothetical homicide on an enemy population.
-ant. underkill.
See REDUNDANCY.

OZONE LAYER. The stratum of the atmosphere that keeps the sport of suntanning from becoming a death-defying act by screening out the ultraviolet rays of the sun. An all-out nuclear exchange could be an ozone slayer, making life on earth impossible.
See NUCLEAR WINTER.

PARANOIA. A path o' logical conviction that nuclear weapons are aimed to kill you. Yossarian, the protagonist of Joseph Heller's novel Catch-22, exhibits the classic paranoid belief that "just because I'm paranoid doesn't mean that they're not out to get me" in the following exchange:

"They're trying to kill me," Yossarian told him calmly.

"No one's trying to kill you," Clevinger cried.

"Then why are they shooting at me?" Yossarian asked.

"They're shooting at <u>everyone</u>," Clevinger answered. "They're trying to kill everyone."

"And what difference does that make?"

And if that wasn't funny, there were lots of things that weren't even funnier."

Don Wright. The Miami News. Reprinted with permission.

PARENTS. People who reproduce the human race by copulation and the arms race by capitulation. Most American parents apparently believe that they protect their children from nuclear war, not by protest, but by sheltering them, first from information, and then from inflammation.

See FALLOUT SHELTER, FIRESTORM.

PARITY. A situation of essential equivalence in nuclear killpower, achieved as soon as our side is "second to none."
--syn. functional equivalence.
See BALANCE OF TERROR, SUPERIORITY.

PATRIOTISM. That love of country which prompts some people to say "America--love it or leave it," and others to say "America--love it and lave it." "To remain silent when your neighbor is boldly persecuted is cowardice," said Abraham Lincoln; "to speak out boldly against injustice, when you are one against many, is the highest patriotism."
See CITIZENS, DEMOCRACY, UN-AMERICAN.

PEACE. 1. According to lexicographer Ambrose Bierce, peace is, "in international relations, a period of cheating between two periods of fighting." 2. According to a play on Pentagonese, peace is "permanent pre-hostility." 3. According to Pope Paul VI, "Peace cannot be limited to a mere absence of war, the result of an ever precarious balance of forces. No, peace is something built up day after day, in the pursuit of an order intended by God, which implies a more perfect form of justice among men and women."
See COLD WAR, JUSTICE.

PEACE THROUGH STRENGTH. The oxymoronic motto that motivates a search for peace with weapons of war.
See CONVERSION.

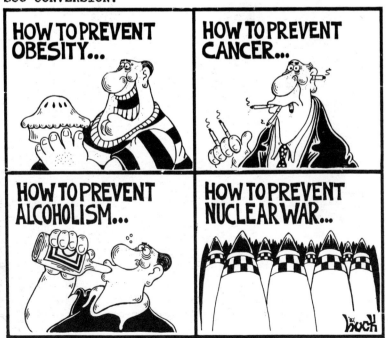

(c) Gary Huck/Rothco.

PEACEKEEPER. Winner of the 1983 Doublespeak Award, President Ronald Reagan's affectionate nickname for the MX missile. Also spelled "Piecekeeper."

QUIZ: PICK THE **TRUE** PEACEKEEPER

Ⓐ M·X   Ⓑ

Reprinted by permission of United Feature Syndicate, Inc.

PEACEMAKER. "Blessed are the peacemakers," said Jesus, who died rather than kill, "for they shall be called the children of God."
--ant. Peacekeeper.
See CIVIL DISOBEDIENCE, PACIFISTS.

PENETRATION AIDS. Also "penaids"; electronic signals or decoy objects broadcast from a missile to help guide the Grim Raper past BMD to his target.

PENTAGON. A five-sided building containing one-dimensional minds, the Pentagon was built by the same man who managed the Manhattan Project. General Groves' motto was "When in doubt, act!"
See DEPARTMENT OF DEFENSE.

PERMANENT DISPOSAL. 1. A fail-safe system of sealing high-level nuclear wastes in geological formations like salt caves, so that they <u>never</u> contaminate the biosphere; 2. The disposition of people to believe this perpetual notion despite 30 years of false promises.
See INTERIM STORAGE, WASTE.

PERMISSIVE ACTION LINKS (PAL). The PAL that prevents the pall; electronic locks that prevent the arming and release of nuclear weapons (except SLBMs) until go-codes are programmed into the mechanisms.
See FAIL-SAFE.

PERSHING II. An American expeditionary force of World War III, namesake of the commander in chief of the American Expeditionary Forces of World War I. Pershing II doubled in cost between March 1981 and June 1982, but was scheduled for production before it was tested, because it might serve as a bargaining chip in Geneva talks limiting inter-mediate range nuclear weapons. Designed to counter the Soviet SS-20, the missile could reach the Soviet Union within 12 minutes.
--syn. Perishing Too.
See ACCIDENTAL WAR, BARGAINING CHIPS, CEP, DESTA-BILIZING WEAPONS, LAUNCH-ON-WARNING, NUCLEAR UMBRELLA, TERCOM.

PESSIMIST. A person who <u>knows</u> that this is the best of all possible worlds.
See IDEALISM, OPTIMIST, REALISM.

PLOWSHARES EIGHT. An octet which premiered a tympanic peace for household hammers and MX missile warheads at a General Electric plant in 1980. Their artistry was unappreciated by the authorities; for their attack on Mark 12-A warheads with sufficient killpower for 3 million people, they were convicted of burglary, criminal mischief, and conspiracy, and were sentenced to jail.
See CIVIL DISOBEDIENCE.

PLUTONIUM. An unnatural element produced as a waste product of nuclear reactors; because plutonium can be used to make atomic bombs, the nuclear industry calls it a "potential nuclear explosive."
See BREEDER, MUF, NUCLEAR REACTOR, NUCLEAR SAFEGUARDS.

PORK BARREL. A container from which Congressmen pull government contracts, money, and jobs for their constituents. This sleight of hand is really slight of ham, since the constituents pay for this legislative legerdemain with their votes, their taxes, and--ultimately--their lives. One of the most notorious political pork barrelers was South Carolina's Mendel Rivers, whose campaign slogan was "Rivers Delivers."
See DEMOCRACY.

POSITIVE CONTROL. Euphemistic substitution for fail-safe, with its implication of possible failure; a policy by which bombers on alert fly to designated points outside Soviet territory and return to base unless voice-ordered to strike.
See FAIL-SAFE.

POST-EXCHANGE RATIOS. Mathematical measures of the
leftovers from a rich menu of Soviet first-strike
and American second-strike options; a comparison
of the nuclear forces available to each side after
a nuclear exchange.
See COUNTERFORCE, NUCLEAR WARFIGHTING.

POST-EXCHANGE RECOVERY SCENARIO. A mourning-after
pill; a script for life after megadeath, set on a
stage strewn with radioactive rubble, and cast
with sick characters in search of a doctor. The
play gives new meaning to the aphorism, "To the
victors belong the spoils."
See SCENARIO.

POST OFFICE. The office of posthumous mail delivery
in the post-attack recovery scenario.

Reprinted with special permission from King Features Syndicate, Inc.

POSTERITY. The descendants whose rights to life we abort by our atomic rites of death.
See PARENTS.

PRECISION-GUIDED MUNITIONS. Smart bombs, which use computers, variable radar frequencies, anti-jamming devices, and other means to zero in on a target and smart the people at ground zero.
See TERCOM.

PREDELEGATION. The American early warring system, a war powers act that extends the President's power to use nuclear weapons to selected military commanders. This policy multiplies the number of fingers on the button, and means things could get out of hand.
--syn. preclearance.
See THE BUTTON.

PRE-EMPTIVE STRIKE. Striking first in order to avoid a first strike.
--syn. anticipatory reaction, anticipatory retaliation, preventive attack.
See FIRST STRIKE.

PRIMATE EQUILIBRIUM PLATFORM. The simian hot seat of an aircraft trainer simulating B-52 flight, in which monkeys are irradiated by the Defense Nuclear Agency to see how well they can "fly" with radiation sickness. After the tests, the monkeys are "euthanized."
See DEFENSE NUCLEAR AGENCY, RADIATION SICKNESS.

PROFIT. The fuel for the fires of the arsonall of democracy.
--ant. prophet.
See MILITARY-INDUSTRIAL COMPLEX.

PROLIFERATION. The legitimate offspring of militarism, nationalism, and nuclear promiscuity, this process of multiplication by addition multiplies chances for nuclear accidents, blackmail, and annihilation by adding more arms in more hands. "Vertical proliferation" refers to the increasing quantity and quality of weapons held by the superpowers; "horizontal proliferation" refers to the increasing number of nations with nuclear weapons. --ant. pro-life.
See NON-PROLIFERATION TREATY.

"Remember The Good Old Days When We Only Worried About Russia Getting One?"

--from Herblock on All Fronts (New American Library, 1980).

PROPAGANDA. Soviet peace proposals. Propagation of American peace proposals, says President Reagan, "is not propaganda. It's public relations."
--syn. public diplomacy.
See CREDIBILITY.

PROXY WAR. A Cold War confrontation in which the superpowers wage war by supplying arms and advisors to allied nations, who donate their territories and citizens to the cause, as in Korea, Vietnam, and Central America.
--syn. austere war.
See COLD WAR.

PSYCHIC NUMBING. The making of numbskulls from the numen of human sensitivity, a deadening process that symptomizes the impact of the Bomb, even berore it hits.
See APATHY, FATALIST, HARDENED.

"Q" CLEARANCE. The highest security clearance of the U.S. government, given to those quislings whose nuclear weapons policies often betray their people for their government.
See SAFEGUARDS.

QUIET DIPLOMACY. A Zen koan, akin to the sound of one hand clapping; President Reagan's description of the sounds or silence in Soviet-American arms control talks, as opposed to the sounds of sirens that could result from the continuing build-ups on both sides.

RACIST. A person who supports an arms race that can destroy whole races--maybe even the human race--without regard to color or creed.
See ARMS RACE, GENOCIDE.

RADIATION. The process by which nuclear energy moves--in waves or particles--from the hypocenter of an explosion to the people on the surface of a sphere called the earth. Direct radiation--in the form of neutrons and gamma rays--occurs immediately and kills people instantaneously. Thermal radiation--or heat--incinerates people near ground zero, and causes third degree burns to exposed people within a wide radius. It also ignites flammable materials, which in turn can ignite people. Fallout radiation distributes the benefits of the explosion more widely, depending on wind and weather conditions.
See FALLOUT, FIRESTORM, NUCLEAR EXPLOSION, RADIATION SICKNESS.

RADIATION SICKNESS. The terminal stage of (p)numania, an epidemic which has ravaged the world since 1945. The immediate symptoms of radiation sickness are nausea, vomiting, and shock. After a latent period of days or weeks, victims experience fever, hair loss, bleeding under the skin, bloody diarrhea, and very low red and white blood counts. Should they survive these symptoms, victims may yet experience delayed effects--either genetic defects (stillbirths, miscarriages, neonatal deaths, retarded and deformed babies, sterility) or malignancies such as leukemia or cancer. The best treatment for radiation sickness is preventive medicine.
See LEUKEMIA, MEDICINE, MICROCEPHALY.

REACTOR. A nuclear generator of electricity, and controversy--over safety, economy, waste-disposal, and potential for proliferation of nuclear power.
--syn. pile.
See BREEDER, NUCLEAR FUEL CYCLE, WASTE.

REAGAN(AT)OMICS. The double-edged sword of Reagan Hood, who robs the poor of social services to pay the military services $1.6 trillion to prepare the way for funeral services.
See HUNGER, REAGANSPEAK.

REAGANSPEAK. The condensed-thought version of the Reader's Digest.
See DOUBLESPEAK, JOKE, REAGAN(AT)OMICS.

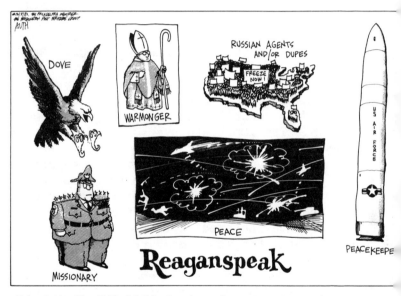

Tony Auth. The Philadelphia Inquirer. Reprinted with permission.

REDUCED RESIDUAL RADIATION (RRR) BOMB. A "blast bomb" that provides so much bang for the buck that it obviates the need to kill residual people with radiation.
--ant. neutron bomb.
See CLEAN BOMB, NEUTRON BOMB.

REALISM. "Realism," says author Jonathan Schell, "is the title given to beliefs whose most notable characteristic is their failure to recognize the chief reality of the age, the pit into which our species threatens to jump."
See IDEALISM, NUCLEAR WAR, PACIFISTS.

REALPOLITIK. Nationalistic power politics that sacrifices the reality principle to "realism."
See BALANCE OF TERROR, NUCLEAR WAR, REALISM.

REDUNDANCY. A literary _faux_ _pas_ but a strategic necessity, redundancy indicates the superfluous weaponry of the superpowers, needed to assure mutually assured destruction.
See MAD, OVERKILL, SUPERPOWER.

REENTRY VEHICLE. A wreckreational vehicle; a surrey with the singe on top; that part of a ballistic missile that reenters the atmosphere with warheads to serve as headsman for the biosphere.
--syn. bus.
See SHROUD, WARHEAD.

REPRESSION. A psychological defense mechanism that allows individuals to "adjust" to social and political repression. Sacrificing our self-respect for respectability, we repress our madness over injustice in order to be diagnosed "normal."
See APATHY, DEFENSE MECHANISM, SCHIZOPHRENIA.

REPROCESSING PLANT. A factory planted to separate the uranium and plutonium of reactor recrement, thus sprouting reactor fuel or "special nuclear material" that could reprocess the planet.
See NUCLEAR FUEL CYCLE, NUCLEAR REACTOR, PLUTONIUM, WASTE.

RESTRICTED DATA. The restrictive clause of the Atomic Energy Act of 1946 which classifies—at the moment of its inception—"any information about the design, manufacture, or use of nuclear weapons," thus subordinating democracy to expertise in atomic energy affairs.
See ATOMIC ENERGY COMMISSION, DEMOCRACY, RETROACTIVE CLASSIFICATION.

RETROACTIVE CLASSIFICATION. A legal concept designed to provide ex post facto justification for the expunction of an expose, as in the government claim that unclassified sources of Howard Morland's 1979 article on how to make an H-bomb were classified.
See RESTRICTED DATA.

SAFEGUARD. A nuclear deodorant with no active ingredients; the euphemistic name for the unworkable ABM system that the U.S. agreed to scrap in SALT I.
See ABM, SALT.

SALT. Strategic Arms Limitation Talks; a rhetorical seasoning that makes human flesh palatable by preserving the arms race. Pronounced with the accent on "Talks."
See ARMS CONTROL, DISARMAMENT, START.

SANE. 1. Mentally healthy, sound of mind, rational; 2. The Committee for a Sane Nuclear Policy; a group formed in 1957 to protest the MADness of atmospheric testing and the balance of terror, and to promote conversion from war to peace.
See APATHY, CONVERSION, DEFENSE MECHANISM, MAD, REPRESSION, SCHIZOPHRENIA.

SCENARIO. A guess in the guise of a hypothesis; a semi-scientific dissimulation game in which a script or possible sequence of actions is dissembled to build a case for the directed use of nuclear weapons; a hot air trial balloon equipped with nuclear weapons.
See LIMITED NUCLEAR WAR, POST-EXCHANGE RECOVERY SCENARIO, THINK TANK, WAR GAMES.

Paul Conrad, 1974, Los Angeles Times. Reprinted with permission.

SCHIZOPHRENIA. Fission for people; the Cold War of the mind; a psychological defense mechanism characterized by withdrawal from reality and splitting of the personality--one half realizes the implications of nuclear weapons and chooses to ignore them, the other half is ignorant of the implications of nuclear weapons and refuses to realize them.
See APATHY, DEFENSE MECHANISM, REPRESSION, SANE.

SCOWCROFT COMMISSION. A committee of MX proponents appointed by President Reagan to find an invulnerable deployment mode for the MX missile. The Scowcroft Commission reported that there was no such mode, but that the US should deploy 100 missiles anyway, to show the Russians that we were serious about making stupid decisions, and to serve as a bargaining chip in future negotiations.
See BARGAINING CHIPS, DENSE PACK, MX, NATIONAL WILL, PEACEKEEPER, WINDOW OF VULNERABILITY.

SECOND STRIKE. The strike before the strike-out; a retaliatory attack. "Second-strike capability" refers to the survivable launchers of unacceptable damage that theoretically prevent both first and second strikes.
See DETERRENCE, FIRST STRIKE, PRE-EMPTIVE STRIKE, SURVIVABILITY, UNACCEPTABLE DAMAGE, VULNERABILITY.

SEMANTICS. Semantic euphemism for "words," as in "I am not going to debate semantics," which means, according to Jonathan Green, "1. I am not going to argue; 2. I am not going to reveal the unpleasant/inadmissible facts behind my hypocritical and inaccurate statement."
See DOUBLESPEAK, EUPHEMISM.

SEVERE DAMAGE. A SACcharine abstraction that severs the damage of bombing from its human and moral context. "Severe damage" means that a target has been reduced to dust; "moderate damage" reduces the target to gravel; while "light damage" leaves rubble on the scene of the crime.
See STRATEGIC AIR COMMAND.

SHOCK WAVE. A shock treatment for the apathetic in which they so-so what's in the wind, and reap the whirlwind. The shock wave of a nuclear explosion causes skull fractures, broken backs, ruptured lungs and eardrums, crushing injuries to the thorax, and massive hemorrhaging. People inside buildings may die as they collapse; people outside may die as their bodies blow (with glass and debris from the busted buildings). The Lovelace Biological and Environmental Research Institute estimates that the "man velocity" of a 165-pound person 3 miles from a 1 megaton explosion will be 30 feet per second, and that there is a 50 percent probability that the body will strike a "hard, flat surface."
See APATHY, BLAST WAVE.

SHOVEL. A dirt-cheap system of civil defense, an implement for getting in a hole. "Everybody's going to make it [through nuclear war] if there are enough shovels to go around," said Deputy Undersecretary of Defense T.K. Jones. "Dig a hole, cover it with a couple of doors and then throw three feet of dirt on top. It's the dirt that does it."
--syn. combat emplacement evacuator.
See CIVIL DEFENSE, DIRT.

ADMINISTRATION'S CIVIL DEFENSE PLAN FOR NUCLEAR WAR

Paul Conrad, 1981, Los Angeles Times. Reprinted with permission.

SHROUD. Conventionally, a cloth used to wrap a corpse for burial; in nuclear newspeak, the covering for MIRV warheads that will rap millions of bodies for burial.
See MIRV.

SILO. Underground cylinder in which the grapes of wrath are stored. In the vernacular, a silo is a pit or tower in which life-sustaining food is preserved; in the looking-glass world of nuclear newspeak, the word refers to a pit that protects the Grim Reaper for dealing death to cannon fodder.
See TUBE.

SIOP. Single Integrated Operating Plan, the US contingency war plans for the operationalized disintegration of a single planet, based in a computer complex of the Underground Command Post in Omaha.
See COMPUTER ERROR, WAR GAMES.

SIN. A violation of the moral law, except the commandment "Thou Shalt Not Kill." Wholesale transgressions of this proscription come under the category of "defense."
See MURDER, TAXES.

SOFT TARGET. Human flesh and its habitats, including cities, factories, ports, airports, depots and camps.
--syn. area target.
--ant. point target.
See AREA BOMBING, COUNTERVALUE.

SOVIET THREAT. The devil of strategic doctrine, which offers hellbent Americans a Mephistophelean motive for the arms race, a claim that--for all escalation--"The Devil made me do it." This Maniachean philosophy gives the devil his due, but also leaves the devil to pay for the devil-may-care build-up of both sides.
--ant. American threat.
See SOVIETIZATION.

--from <u>Jules Feiffer's America</u> (Random House, 1982).

SOVIETIZATION. 1. The brutal process by which the USSR subdues its satellites; 2. The futile process by which the United States imitates Soviet militarism to preserve freedom and democracy.
See DUPE, SOVIET THREAT, UN-AMERICAN.

(c) Gary Huck/Rothco.

PACE RACE. 1. One small step for man, one giant leap for ICBMs; the public face of the arms race in the 1960s; a missile marathon designed to shoot the moon before shooting the earth; **2.** The rush for shelter space after the onset of nuclear war.

SPENT FUEL. The depleted "fissile material" of a nuclear reactor, called "spent" because of the money spent to discover, mine, enrich, reprocess, and store it until it becomes innocuous.
See INTERIM STORAGE, PERMANENT DISPOSAL, WASTE.

STABLE DETERRENCE. The balance-of-terror stalemat that discourages use of nuclear weapons withou discouraging build-up of nuclear arsenals.
See BALANCE OF TERROR, DETERRENCE, STRATEGIC STA BILITY.

STAR WARS. 1. The $9.5 million dollar 1977 movie i which the forces of good use intelligence an courage to triumph over the technologica superiority of the Evil Empire; 2. The $26 billio dollar 1983 scenario of a movie actor in which th forces of good use superior (although untested an destabilizing) death stars to defeat the "evi empire" of the USSR.
--syn. strategic defense initiative.
See ABM, BMD, DESTABILIZING WEAPONS.

START. A SALT substitute; 1982 acronym for Strategi Arms Reduction Talks; to date, a false start fc disarmament. "In its first year," said John New house, "the Reagan administration did next t nothing about the SALT process except change it name." In subsequent years, it did less.
See ARMS CONTROL, DISARMAMENT, REAGANSPEAK, SALT.

STEALTH. The sneak purview of a new American bombe (for the 1990s) with a design and composition tha makes it virtually invisible to radar.
--syn. advanced technology bomber.
See B-1, HEAVY BOMBER.

STERILITY MONEY. 1. According to Jonathan Gree "extra pay given to submariners who risk tl dangers of leaky nuclear reactors"; 2. The taxe we pay to produce the potent weapons that ma render the earth barren.
See ECOCIDE, MUTATION.

STOCKPILE. 1. According to Webster, "a reserve supply of something essential accumulated within a country for use during a shortage"; 2. The strategic reserve; a reservation for doomsday at the Holocaust Inn. Combined Soviet-American stockpiles contain the explosive equivalent of 13 billion tons of TNT--equal to a million Hiroshima bombs; 3. The heap of dead livestock succeeding nuclear war and preceding human starvation.
See BALANCE OF TERROR.

STRATEGIC AIR COMMAND (SAC). The SACerdotal priesthood of people whose vocation is to prepare human sacrifice and the sack of civilizations in the name of the gods of war--Atlas, Nike, Poseidon, and Zeus, among others.
See LOOKING GLASS, SEVERE DAMAGE.

STRATEGIC COUPLING. The _coitus_ _eruptus_ by which Soviet penetration of Western Europe is met by a thrust of US strategic forces, leading in due course to the coming of spasm war.
--syn. tripwire.
See AUTOMATICISM, ESCALATION LADDER.

STRATEGIC DOCTRINE. Theory that deals with deterrence, with the warfighting that follows the failure of deterrence, but not with the failure of warfighting.
See EXPERT, THINK TANK.

STRATEGIC STABILITY. An imaginary condition of echinate equilibrium in which neither superpower feels threatened or pressured to increase or modernize its nuclear arsenal.
--syn. arms race stability.
See CRISIS STABILITY, STABLE DETERRENCE.

STRATEGIC WARNING. 1. A warning of the onset o
nuclear war that comes early enough to be appreci
ated months or weeks before the country is depre
ciated. A "tactical warning" comes later--onl
days or hours before an attack; 2. The warning o
protesters that strategic doctrine likely leads t
strategic warning and to strategic warring.
See CIVIL DEFENSE.

STRATEGIC WEAPONS. Long-range weapons (able to hi
the enemy's homeland); a thoughtful sound fo
thoughtless weapons, designed to make the use o
intercontinental delivery systems seem rational
scientific, and discretionary.
See TACTICAL NUCLEAR WEAPONS.

SUFFICIENCY. 1. Enough; 2. The number of survivabl
warheads sufficient to deter the enemy by destroy
ing the enemy's society, a number that increase
as fast as our capacity to make warheads--sinc
1971, about three a day. Asked what sufficienc
means, a former Deputy Defense Secretary answered
"It is a good word to use in a speech. Beyon
that, it doesn't mean a goddamned thing."
See OVERKILL, REDUNDANCY.

SUICIDE. First-person first-degree murder; the ne
plus ultra of selflessness. In 1981 the America
Association of Suicidology noted that "much lik
an individual bent on self-destruction, whose ris
of suicide increases significantly once he ha
chosen a method of suicide, and acquired th
necessary means to carry out the method, the worl
community of mankind currently faces an extremel
high risk of self-destruction having chose
nuclear holocaust as the method, and havin
acquired and having immediately available nuclea

weapons in such quantity as to instantly eliminate
life on earth."
See ECOCIDE, GENOCIDE, MURDER.

UICIDE JOCKEYS. 1. The CB "handle" for the truckers
who drive 8 million miles annually delivering missile warheads and components from the Pantex plant
in Amarillo, Texas, to about 125 sites in the 48
contiguous states; 2. The rest of us, who "keep on
truckin'" in the arms race.
--syn. couriers.
See WHITE TRAIN.

UNSHINE UNIT. A shady semantic cover for the ratio
of strontium-90 to normal calcium in people
exposed to weapons test fallout.
See RADIATION, RADIATION SICKNESS.

UPERIORITY. A position of strength that allows one
country to begin negotiations to achieve a parity
that would not threaten its well-deserved
superiority; a margin of safety from sensibility.
In 1974, Henry Kissinger observed that "one of the
questions we have to ask ourselves as a country is
what in the name of God is strategic superiority?
. . . What can you do with it?" The Report of the
Secretary of Defense for fiscal year 1983 claims
that the "modernization program is not designed to
achieve nuclear 'superiority' for the United
States, [but] by the same token, we will make
every necessary effort to prevent the Soviet Union
from acquiring such superiority and to insure the
margin of safety for our own security."

"In the real world," responds Noel Gayler
"'superiority' has no meaning. We and Russia are
like two riverboat gamblers sitting across a green
table, each with a gun pointed at the other's
belly and each gun on hair trigger. The size of
the guns doesn't make much difference; if either
weapon is used, both gamblers are dead."
--syn. margin of safety.
See BALANCE OF TERROR, PARITY.

SUPERPOWER. 1. Abbreviated version of superfluous
power; any nation with overkill capability; 2. The
US or the USSR, a dyad devoted to dying.
See NUCLEAR CLUB, OVERKILL.

SURGICAL STRIKE. Medicinal euphemism for precision
bombing designed to cut out military tumors on the
enemy's body politic without killing the patient
or trying his patience. The operation is con-
ducted from great distances; consequently the
bombing is almost as imprecise as the bombast.
--ant. area bombing.
See AREA BOMBING, COUNTERFORCE.

SURVIVABILITY. The ability of weapons systems, not
people, to withstand a first strike in order to
respond and kill people, not weapons systems.
Possession of a survivable force that can wreak
"unacceptable damage" on the enemy is the sine qua
non of deterrence.
--syn. second strike capability.
--ant. vulnerability.
See DETERRENCE, SECOND STRIKE.

SURVIVALISM. Asocial Darwinism, the survival of the fatuous; those who outfit themselves--not to prevent nuclear war--but for the fitting fate of slow starvation, radiation sickness, genetic mutation, and nuclear winter in the post-attack recovery scenario.
See FATALIST, MUTATION, NUCLEAR WINTER, POST-ATTACK RECOVERY SCENARIO, RADIATION SICKNESS.

SURVIVOR. In nuclear war, a person whose physiological functions persist beyond the culture that gives those functions human meaning; a person who outlives human life.
See SURVIVABILITY, SURVIVALISM.

TACTICAL NUCLEAR WEAPONS. Tactless tactics; atomic bombs deployed mainly in Europe to protect NATO from Soviet advances, "tactical" only in the sense that they are part of battlefield maneuvers. Tactical weapons usually have a short range (100 miles or less) and a small yield (up to the equivalent of eight Hiroshima bombs). Morton Halperin, former deputy assistant secretary of defense, summarized the etiquette of tactical nuclear weapons: "The NATO doctrine is that we will fight with conventional forces until we are losing, then we fight with tactical nuclear weapons until we are losing, and then we will blow up the world."
See LIMITED NUCLEAR WAR, NEUTRON BOMB, NUCLEAR UMBRELLA, THEATRE NUCLEAR FORCES.

TAXES. Death on the installment plan, a metho
whereby we pay for war while we pray for peace
Benjamin Franklin observed that only two thing
are inevitable--death and taxes. It is the spe
cial genius of the modern age to use one to assur
the other.
See CITIZENS, DEMOCRACY.

(c) 1985, Los Angeles Times Syndicate. Reprinted with permission.

TAX RESISTANCE. The Resistance movement of the Col
War, inspired by the slogan "No Taxation Withou
Reprehension"; a group of people engaged in th
struggle for national liberation in a countr
under military (pre)occupation. "Form 1040 is th
place where the Pentagon enters all of our lives
and asks our unthinking cooperation with the idc
of nuclear destruction," observes Resistanc
leader Raymond Hunthausen. "I think the teachir
of Jesus tells us to render to a nuclear-arme
Caesar what that Caesar deserves--tax resistance.
See BISHOPS, TAXES.

TECHNOLOGICAL ANTICIPATION. The infeariority complex of nuclear strategists; the assumption that "whatever we can conceive they will deploy." "There is no better way of increasing the military budget," claims analyst Edward Bottome, "than that of convincing the Congress of some _future_ threat to American security by the Soviet _capability_ to produce a weapon system."
See TECHNOLOGICAL IMPERATIVE, WORST-CASE SCENARIO.

TECHNOLOGICAL IMPERATIVE. The _deus_ _est_ _machina_ of atomic armament by which invention becomes the mother of necessity, and know-how leads nowhere. "There is a kind of mad momentum to the development of all nuclear weaponry," said Robert McNamara. "If a weapons system works--and works well--there is strong pressure from many directions to procure and deploy the weapon out of all proportion to the prudent level required."
See INTERSERVICE RIVALRY.

TELEMETRY. The telltale art of telling testers the measurements of missile performance.
See ENCRYPTION, TESTING.

TERCOM. Terrain Contour Matching, a computer matching service that plays Cupid (and Thanatos) for nuclear missiles and their targets. The guidance system's computer contains a map of its target, which it matches with photographs taken during flight, in order to keep on course. Both Pershing II and the cruise missile have TERCOM systems.
--syn. terminal guidance.
See CRUISE MISSILE, PERSHING.

TESTING. Nuclear bombing without nuclear war; a process of experimental trial by fire. Before 1963, testing contaminated the atmosphere; current tests take place only in the underworld, and thus contaminate only international relations.

Each of the American tests is named by a "weapons information specialist" in the Department of Energy, who nixes words that are controversial. A 1981 memo noted that "words should not be submitted for approval that connote or imply by their meaning aggressiveness, a relation to war, weapons, explosives, the military, potentially sensitive situations or other categories that in some way reflect on weapons programs."
See COMPREHENSIVE TEST BAN, LIMITED TEST BAN, MODERNIZATION.

THEATER. 1. A playhouse; 2. The setting for the staging of a limited nuclear war; 3. Europe.
See LIMITED NUCLEAR WAR, TACTICAL NUCLEAR WEAPONS.

THEATER NUCLEAR FORCES. Nuclear weapons booked for an exclusive engagement in a single theatre, usually Europe. Theatre nuclear forces include tactical, intermediate-range, and Eurostrategic weapons.
See STRATEGIC WEAPONS, TACTICAL NUCLEAR WEAPONS, THEATER.

THINK TANK. A self-propelled combat vehicle armored with ersatz expertise and equipped with cannon and machine guns that fire scenarios and jargon across the intellectual landscape; an independent research institute that usually depends on government contracts.
See EXPERT, SCENARIO.

THREE MILE ISLAND. A derailed LOCA-motive: the <u>locus</u> of a nuclear catastrophe that stopped only 30 minutes from meltdown; and the <u>motive</u> for a reconsideration of the fantastic safety claims of the nuclear industry.
See LOCA, MELTDOWN, NORMAL ABERRATION.

THREE MILE ISLAND REPORT

--from <u>Herblock</u> <u>on</u> <u>All</u> <u>Fronts</u> (New American Library, 1980).

THROW WEIGHT. The capacity of missiles to uplift warheads that rain down destruction on the enemy--usually measured in pounds; the maximum weight (of the guidance systems, warheads, and penetration aids) that has been flight-tested on the boost stages of a missile.
See YIELD.

TIME-URGENT HARD TARGET KILL CAPABILITY. The nuclear variation of one-hour cleaning; a measure of the ability to destroy enemy silos, submarines, and bomber fields before their weapons set out to destroy ours.
See FIRST STRIKE, HARD TARGET, HARD TARGET CAPABILITY.

TITAN II. According to Colonel Frank Horton of the Grand Forks Air Force Base (N.D.), the Titan II is "a very large, potentially disruptive reentry system." Such clarity of expression in describing America's largest and most lethal ICBM won second place for Horton in the balloting for the 1983 Doublespeak Award.
See BALLISTIC MISSILE.

TOTAL WAR. The state or condition of international relations that totals the world.
--syn. all-out strategic exchange.
See WORLD WAR III.

TRIAD. The Holy Trinity of the deterrence deity, consisting of ICBMs, submarines, and bombers, each of which can wreak unacceptable damage by transubstantiating the enemy.
See DETERRENCE, SURVIVABILITY, UNACCEPTABLE DAMAGE, WEAPONS MIX.

TRIDENT. 1. The devil's pitchforce; a nuclear submarine with 24 MIRVed SLBMs and about 200 warheads
each eight times more powerful than the Hiroshima
bomb; 2. A missile (D-5 Trident II) which, with
navigational fixes from NAVSTAR satellites, has a
superb CEP and counterforce capability. Despite
destabilizing first-strike capabilities like MX,
Trident's survivability has assured its survivability in Congress.
--syn. boomer (applies to Poseidon too).
See DESTABILIZING WEAPONS.

TRUST. The uncommon coin of the confidence games
played with nuclear weapons. We do not trust the
Russians. We inscribe our coins to say "In God We
Trust," but we invest our coins to say otherwise.
--ant. deterrence.
See JUSTICE.

TRUTH. See CREDIBILITY, PROPAGANDA.

TUBE. The cylinder from which SLBMs are fired to
knock people and property down the tubes.
See SILO, TRIDENT.

UNACCEPTABLE DAMAGE. A euphemism for genocide,
specifically the quantity of death and destruction
that keeps nuclear powers from attacking one
another. Secretary of Defense Robert McNamara
operationalized the idea of unacceptable damage by
saying that U.S. second-strike weapons should be
able to destroy "one fifth to one fourth of her
population and one half of her industrial capacity."
--ant. acceptable damage.
See COUNTERVALUE, DETERRENCE, MASSIVE RETALIATION,
OVERKILL, REDUNDANCY.

'GREAT NEWS ! WE'VE INFLICTED UNACCEPTABLE DAMAGE ON THE OTHER SIDE.'

Tony Auth. The Philadelphia Inquirer. Reprinted with permission.

UN-AMERICAN. 1. A person--usually an American--who rejects the proposition "Better dead than Red" without necessarily accepting the opposite; 2. A person--usually an American--unable to believe, as do other Americans, that the United States must violate its principles in order to preserve them. See BETTER DEAD THAN RED, DUPE, IDEALISM.

UNILATERAL DISARMAMENT. A politically suicidal process of reducing the chances of genocide and ecocide by reducing the number of nuclear weapons. Unlike arms control (or even the nuclear freeze), unilateral disarmament follows the dictum of retired Admiral Noel Gayler, who said that "the way to get rid of nuclear weapons is to get rid of nuclear weapons."
See ARMS CONTROL, DISARMAMENT.

UNITED STATES. Us. Said Pogo, "We have met the enemy and he is us."
See CITIZENS, ENEMY, SOVIET THREAT.

UNTHINK. A verb constructed in strict conformity to George Orwell's "Principles of Newspeak." To think is, according to Webster, "to form or have in the mind; conceive." To unthink, then, is "to deform or heave from the mind; deceive."
See DOUBLESPEAK, REAGANSPEAK, THE UNTHINKABLE.

THE UNTHINKABLE. 1. Nuclear holocaust, the final product of a process of thinking nothing of using nuclear weapons to win a war; 2. Peace.
See ECOCIDE, INNOCENT BYSTANDER, PEACE.

VERIFICATION. The truth or consequences of arms control; the process of discovering how the enemy is violating an arms control agreement. During the 1950s, the U.S. insisted on on-site inspection for verification; consequently there were no treaties to verify. With the development of national technical means of verification (esp. spy satellites) it became possible to verify agreements controlling testing, ABM systems, and missile launchers without on-site inspections. With START proposals for controlling warheads, and with new technology such as Midgetman and cruise missiles, verification may again block bargaining.
See ARMS CONTROL, NATIONAL TECHNICAL MEANS, SALT.

VITAL INTERESTS. Interests (often economic) that we would kill for.
See NATIONAL INTEREST.

VLADIVOSTOK ACCORDS. SALT I 1/2; a 1974 arms control "agreement in principle" between U.S. President Gerald Ford and Soviet Premier Leonid Breshnev, permitting the US and the USSR to triple the number of warheads they already possessed.
See ARMS CONTROL, SALT.

VULNERABILITY. According to Webster, the state or condition of being able to be wounded; the human condition. In strategic semantics, vulnerability is the state or condition of missiles, bombers, or submarines that calls into question their ability to respond to a first strike with unacceptable damage to the enemy. Strategic invulnerability is, therefore, a threat to human vulnerability.
--ant. survivability.
See CRISIS STABILITY, SURVIVABILITY, UNACCEPTABLE DAMAGE, WINDOW OF VULNERABILITY.

WAR GAMES. The national sport; a ritual pre-enactment of an important rite of passage among Americans--namely death. In 1982, the US Navy began to use video computers to train people to fight and win a nuclear war. "We've found that it's a lot of fun," reported a Navy Lieutenant Commander. "An awful lot of people find it just as addictive as Pac-Man."
--syn. doomsday scenarios.
See GAME THEORY, SCENARIO.

WARHEAD. 1. The explosive part of projectiles like bombs or missiles; 2. The head of state.
--syn. payload.
See DELIVERY VEHICLE.

WAR TERMINATION. Ending the war to end all wars, either by surrender or negotiation--which is unlikely, since both sides intend to decapitate command and control systems--or, more likely, by extermination. According to Herbert Scoville, the problem of war termination is that no one knows how to stop a nuclear war because no one knows how to lose."
See C3I, DECAPITATION, ESCALATION, WIN.

WASTE. 1. The bomb program; 2. Radioactive byproducts of the nuclear fuel cycle, including uranium tailings from milling and enrichment, and spent fuel from nuclear reactors. High-level wastes are so radioactive that they will kill proximate people, so they must be stored until they become innocuous--in the case of plutonium, for example, about half a million years; 3. Nuclear reactors that must be decommissioned after 30 or 40 years of operation. Beginning in the 1990s, radioactive reactors must be mothballed, entombed in concrete, or dismantled, at what cost no one knows; 4 The human effort dedicated to composing and disposing of these wastes. According to the Vatican, "the waste involved in the overproduction of military devices and the extent of unsatisfied vital needs is in itself an act of aggression against the victims of it. For even when they are not used, by their cost alone, armaments kill the poor by causing them to starve."
See NUCLEAR FUEL CYCLE, REACTOR.

WEAPONS MIX. A pre-packaged set of ingredients for a devil's food wake; the number and proportion of different weapons in the arsenal of a nation; the "optimum mix" balances bombers, land-based missiles, and submarine-based missiles.
See FORCE STRUCTURE, TRIAD.

WHITE TRAIN. A once-white freight train fraught wit
the new Black Death; the delivery vehicle whic
mainlines warheads from the Pantex assembly plar
in Amarillo, Texas to weapons depots around tl
country.
See SUICIDE JOCKEYS.

WIN. To destroy a civilization, perhaps civilizatic
itself. Defining "victory," an Undersecretary c
Defense for Research and Engineering said that "j
escalation cannot be controlled, then our objec
tive is to maximize the resultant economic ar
military power of the U.S. relative to the enen
in the post-war period by destroying targets crit
ical to enemy postwar power and recovery."]
1960, SAC commander Tommy Powers rendered thj
idea in plain English. "Look," he said. "At tl
end of the war, if there are two Americans and or
Russian, we win!"

Robert S. McNamara claimed that "we cannot win
nuclear war, a strategic nuclear war, in the nor
mal sense of the word 'win.'" Caspar Weinberge
agreed in 1982 that nuclear war was unwinnable
but added that "we certainly are planning not t
be defeated." "You show me a Secretary of Defens
who's planning not to prevail," he said with unin
peachable logic, "and I'll show you a Secretary c
Defense who ought to be impeached."
--syn. die, prevail.

WINDOW OF VULNERABILITY. The rhetorical lookin
glass that magnifies the Soviet threat and minir
izes the American arsenal; a pane of gas throu
which one sees the transparent lie that Rona]
Reagan used to make MX critics vulnerable to po]
itical pressure; an imaginary open window throu

which the Soviets could shoot ICBMs to destroy our ICBMs. This fenestral phenomenon was expected to occur in the mid-1980s, but it did not. The window opened rhetorically during 1979 SALT II hearings, opened wider with Reagan's mouth in 1981 and 1982, but was closed by the President's 1983 Scowcroft Commission, which said that land-based ICBMs were not vulnerable.

'WINDOW OF VULNERABILITY'

Paul Conrad, 1981, Los Angeles Times. Reprinted with permission.

The imaginary window did, however, have som
shattering results. The President proposed t
develop and deploy MX missiles to make Sovie
ICBMs vulnerable to a first strike. And in hi
START proposal, Reagan also suggested that th
Soviets reduce their inventory of threatenin
ICBMs, apparently on the assumption that peopl
who live in glass houses shouldn't stow stones.
See BOMBER GAP, CREDIBILITY, CREDULOUS, MIDGETMAN
MISSILE GAP, MX, SCOWCROFT COMMISSION, START, VUL
NERABILITY.

WORLD WAR II. The first nuclear war. "The mos
important fact about World War II," said Lewi
Mumford, "is that in the course of fighting it th
ancient art of warfare gave way to the increasin
practice of genocide. Following the theory an
practice of our Fascist enemies, whose mora
nihilism destroyed the very principle of res
traint, the democratic powers took over genocid
or mass extermination."
See WORLD WAR III, WORLD WAR IV, etc.

WORLD WAR III. The blight at the end of the tunnel
the war to end all wars, to make the world saf
for entomology.
See TOTAL WAR.

WORST-CASE SCENARIO. A self-fulfilling prophecy; th
nightmare of imaginary horribles for which w
prepare daily by constructing equally horribl
realities. "It is the business of military stra
tegists to prepare for all eventualities," sai
theologian Reinhold Neibuhr, "and it is the fata
error of such strategists to create the eventuali
ties for which they must prepare."
See ARMS RACE, SCENARIO.

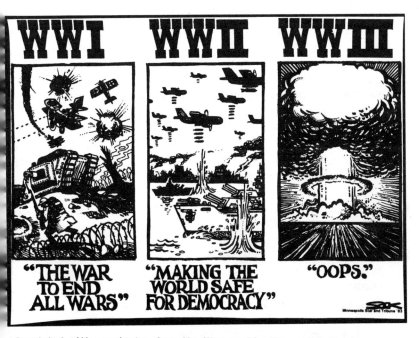

Reprinted with permission from the Minneapolis Star and Tribune.

IELD. The bang for the buck; the explosive force--
expressed in tons of TNT--of a bomb designed to
bang up the enemy and make him yield.
See KILOTON, MEGATON.

HE ZERO OPTION. A 1981 Reagan proposal to cancel
deployment of US Pershing II missiles in Europe in
return for Soviet dismantling 600 intermediate
range missiles (including new SS-20s) with 1,200
warheads, so called because it would eliminate
IRBMs in Europe, and because the United States
would sacrifice nothing to get the Soviet Union to
dismantle several hundred missiles. Not surpris-
ingly, the zero option has produced zero results.
See BARGAINING CHIPS, CRUISE MISSILE, PERSHING.

A FEW GOOD SOURCES FOR FURTHER READING

I. On Language:

George Orwell, "Politics and the English Language," in Shooting an Elephant (New York: Harcourt Brace, 1950)

Jonathan Green, Newspeak: A Dictionary of Jargon (London: Routledge & Kegan Paul, 1984)

Stephen Hilgartner et. al., Nukespeak: The Selling of Nuclear Technology in America (San Francisco: Sierra Club Books, 1982)

Hugh Rank, ed., Language and Public Policy (Urbana, IL: National Council of Teachers of English, 1974)

William Safire, Safire's Political Dictionary (New York: Ballantine Books, 1978)

Hugh Rawson, A Dictionary of Euphemisms and Other Doubletalk (New York: Crown Publishers, 1981)

Neil Postman, Charles Weingartner, and Terence P. Moran, ed., Language in America (New York: Pegasus, 1969)

The Quarterly Review of Doublespeak
--available for $3.00 a year from the National Council of Teachers of English, 1111 Kenyon Rd. Urbana, IL 61801

II. On Nuclear Issues

Jack Dennis, ed., The Nuclear Almanac: Confronting the Atom in War and Peace (Reading, MA: Addison-Wesley, 1984)

Sandra Sedacca, Up in Arms (Washington: Common Cause, 1984)

Michael Stephenson and John Weal, Nuclear Dictionary (Burnt Mill: Longman, 1985)

Teena Mayers, Understanding Nuclear Weapons and Arms Control (Arlington, VA: Arms Control Research, 1983)

Fred Kaplan, The Wizards of Armageddon (New York: Simon & Schuster, 1983)

Richard Smoke, National Security and the Nuclear Dilemma (Reading, MA: Addison-Wesley, 1984)

Lawrence Freedman, The Evolution of Nuclear Strategy (New York: St. Martin's Press, 1983)

Thomas B. Cochran, William M. Arkin, and Milton M. Hoenig, Nuclear Weapons Databook (Cambridge, MA: Ballinger, 1984)

Freeman Dyson, Weapons and Hope (New York: Harper & Row, 1984)

Bulletin of the Atomic Scientists
--a monthly journal available for $22.50 a year from 5801 S. Kenwood, Chicago, IL 60637

THE AUTHOR

James J. Farrell is assistant professor of History
and American Studies at St. Olaf College in North-
field, Minnesota, where he teaches a course on
"Nuclear Weapons and American Culture." His first
book, Inventing the American Way of Death 1830-
1920, earned him the nickname "Dr. Death." For
his current research, students have dubbed him
"Dr. Megadeath." All things considered, he
prefers life.

THE PRESS

Frank Lloyd Wright used the word "Usonia" as a
short form of "the United States of America." He
disliked the linguistic imperialism of "America,"
which takes the name of two continents to charac-
terize one country. Usonia Press takes its
inspiration from individuals like Frank Lloyd
Wright, whose criticism of the architectural trad-
itions of his time allowed him to build structures
better imbedded in the foundation of American
ideas and ideals. Usonia Press also attempts to
publish books that exemplify the complexity of
Wright's own thought: "To think 'in simple' is to
deal in simples , and that means with an eye single to the altogether."

The Nuclear
Devil's Dictionary

Order Form

Please send ___ copies of
The Nuclear Devil's Dictionary to:

Name:_____

Address:_____

_____

_____

Enclosed is $_____.
$7.95 postpaid. Minnesota residents add 6% sales
Satisfaction guaranteed.

Usonia Press
Box 19440-A
Diamond Lake Station
Minneapolis, MN 55419

The Nuclear
Devil's Dictionary

Order Form

Please send ___ copies of
The Nuclear Devil's Dictionary to:

Name:_____

Address:_____

_____

_____

Enclosed is $_____.
$7.95 postpaid. Minnesota residents add 6% sales
Satisfaction guaranteed.

                    Usonia Press
                    Box 19440-A
                 Diamond Lake Station
                 Minneapolis, MN 55419